Together

MISSIONAL WISDOM LIBRARY
RESOURCES FOR CHRISTIAN COMMUNITY

The Missional Wisdom Foundation experiments with and teaches about alternative forms of Christian community. The definition of what constitutes a Christian community is shifting as many seek spiritual growth outside of the traditional confines of church. Christians are experimenting with forming communities around gardens, recreational activities, coworking spaces, and hundreds of other focal points, connecting with their neighbors while being aware of the presence of God in their midst. The Missional Wisdom Library series includes resources that address these kinds of communities and their cultural, theological, and organizational implications.

Series Editor: Larry Duggins

> vol. 1: *Missional. Monastic. Mainline.: A Guide to Starting Missional Micro-Communities in Historically Mainline Traditions*, by Elaine A. Heath and Larry Duggins

Forthcoming titles

> *The Julian Way: Towards a Theology of Fulness for All of God's People*, by Justin Hancock

> *What Kind of God? Reading the Bible with a Missional Church*, edited by Bret Wells

> *Simple Harmony: Thoughts on Holistic Christian Life*, revised edition, by Larry Duggins

> *Virtuous Friendship: The New Testament, Grego-Roman Friendship Language, and Contemporary Community*, by Douglas A. Hume

Together

Community as a Means of Grace

Larry Duggins

CASCADE *Books* · Eugene, Oregon

TOGETHER
Community as a Means of Grace

Missional Wisdom Library: Resources for Christian Community 2

Cascade Books
An Imprint of Wipf and Stock Publishers
199 W. 8th Ave., Suite 3
Eugene, OR 97401

www.wipfandstock.com

PAPERBACK ISBN: 978-1-5326-1305-0
HARDCOVER ISBN: 978-1-5326-1307-4
EBOOK ISBN: 978-1-5326-1306-7

Cataloguing-in-Publication data:

Names: Duggins, Larry, author.

Title: Together : community as a means of grace / Larry Duggins.

Description: Eugene, OR : Cascade Books, 2017 | Missional Wisdom Library: Resources for Christian Community | Includes bibliographical references.

Identifiers: ISBN 978-1-5326-1305-0 (paperback) | ISBN 978-1-5326-1307-4 (hardcover) | ISBN 978-1-5326-1306-7 (ebook)

Subjects: LCSH: Christian life.

Classification: BV4517.5 D84 2017 (paperback) | BV4517.5 D84 (ebook)

Manufactured in the U.S.A.   04/25/17

Contents

Introduction

As I AM WRITING this, the Missional Wisdom Foundation (MWF) is undertaking two grand experiments in community. One is repurposing the large fellowship hall and basement of a mostly empty church building in Dallas into a flexible coworking space. We are creating places for entrepreneurs and work-at-home folks to gather and network together. We are renovating the church kitchen space into a full-featured commercial kitchen, allowing neighborhood food businesses to share a "creative space" to expand their businesses and share ideas and equipment. The large concrete-block classrooms are being transformed into specialized spaces. One houses sewing machines for a cooperative of refugees from Africa, another is a dance studio, a third will become a recording studio for podcasts and video blogs, and the future of the fourth is still unknown. When the project comes together, around one hundred people will be sharing the space in ways no one would have anticipated even five years ago.

In a small church in Asheville, North Carolina, we are working to transform the building into a community common space that is used every day of the week. We will build out a coworking space and a creative space there too, but in this location, we will also remove all of the pews from the sanctuary to make it a flexible community meeting space while retaining its status as a place of worship. The old chancel area will become a flexible, living room–like teaching space, and ramps will be added and bathrooms updated to make the entire building disability accessible.

Introduction

The parsonage next door will be home to quilting and sewing groups, and the garage will become a woodworking shop. An entire classroom will house items from the church's past in a museum display to honor the church's heritage, while other classrooms will be flexibly designed for conferences, classes, and Sunday school meetings. The MWF will host seminars and college and seminary immersion experiences in the space, while housing the participants in the expanded parsonage. A sidewalk will be built from the church parking lot to the elementary school behind the church to encourage people to "take a shortcut" through the church property to relieve a bit of parking congestion at the school. The new playground and gardens along the sidewalk will encourage them to linger a bit, if they have the time.

So, as we undertake these adventures, we are encountering people who look at all these activities and ask, "How is *this* church?" They question our ability to remain a nonprofit organization when we charge for using our spaces. They wonder how these activities are different from executive suites where people share a secretary and a copy machine. They want to know if we are sneaking a commercial business into their residential neighborhood.

And if they are Christian people they also wonder about how people will come to know God in such a place. Will everyone be required to attend a Bible study? Will there be a pastor? How will people encounter Jesus without a hymnbook or a sermon?

Those questions called this book into being, but there was more. The three of us who were leading the MWF at the time—Dr. Elaine Heath (now dean of the Duke Divinity School), Dr. Bret Wells (pastor, coach, and distance learning expert), and me—all independently began to be bothered by Matthew 18:20: "For where two or three are gathered in my name, I'm there with them." We were struck by the universality of this statement; Jesus was present wherever two or three people were gathered. Did that include work? Soccer practice? Starbucks? The movies? As we struggled with that idea, Elaine refocused us on the phrase "in my name." What exactly did it mean to be gathered in his name? Were we gathered in his name when we sat together in a meeting room

viii

discussing these ideas? Could be we gathered in his name and do other things too?

After working on these ideas together for a while, the Wesleyan in me began to emerge and we began to think about being together as a means of grace. Is it possible that the very act of being together opens a path for the Holy Spirit to connect with us? And, through that connection, transform "two or three gathered" into "two or three gathered in his name"?

This book examines these questions. We will begin by considering three interrelated theological steps. The first step encounters the nature of God as Trinity and probes the significance of that concept. The second step considers the nature of humanity and our place as part of creation and how our nature relates to community. The third step ponders community as an important link between God and humanity. Working from that theological base, we will consider various kinds of Christian community and how they can work to bring people closer to God and each other.

The Trinity: God Is Community

THE CONCEPT OF THE Trinity is hard for many of us to grasp. Many visualize God the Father as the stern guy with the big white beard, gruffly judging people or sitting on a giant golden throne floating on fluffy, white clouds. Most can conjure up an image of Jesus from the picture that hung on the wall of a Sunday school classroom—shoulder-length, curly brown hair, vaguely Caucasian, deep blue eyes. The Holy Spirit, or, even stranger, the Holy Ghost, is often an obscure idea: a nebulous force that makes those people at that other church do crazy things like waving their arms in the air or speaking in tongues. And the whole business about how the three of them are actually one? Well, that just doesn't add up!

The concept of the Trinity is further complicated by how we choose to name the three persons of the Trinity. We struggle to find words to call them: Father, Son, Holy Spirit; God, Jesus, Spirit; Creator, Redeemer, Sustainer; Beyond Them, With Them, Within Them; Lover, Beloved, Love. Is God the First Person of the Trinity or all three of them together? These names imply interrelatedness, connection, and interaction, but some of them also imply gender, role, and hierarchy. The whole notion of the Trinity is abstract and can be quite confusing and uncomfortable. The idea of the Trinity is so mysterious and alien that we have difficulty even finding names for the seemingly unnameable.

Yet in the view of many Christian readers, the idea of the Trinity, God as three in one, appears from the very beginning of the Bible. In Genesis 1:1, God creates—an act that traditionally defines the First Person of the Trinity. In Genesis 1:2, it is the Spirit of God—the *ruach* in Hebrew—that sweeps across the face of the waters, calling forth the image of the Third Person of the Trinity. In Genesis 1:3, the Word of God is spoken, calling forth the light that illumines creation and becoming the name that the Apostle John uses for Jesus at the beginning of his Gospel. The very first actions of God that we encounter in scripture are acts of community: the Creator, the Word, and the Spirit moving together, calling creation into being.

The Hebrew Scriptures are sometimes thought to associate war, law, and judgment with God. In the first dozen chapters of Genesis, that all-powerful God exiles Cain for killing his brother, floods the earth because of the sinfulness of humanity, and encounters Abram and sends him off to a new land. This terrifying God seems to be judge, jury, and executioner. Yet even in early scripture, as humanity comes to grips with who God is and how to relate to God, glimpses of the Trinity and a different face of God peek through. When Abraham (God changes Abram's name to Abraham in Genesis 17) encounters God at the Oak of Mamre, as described in Genesis 18, he finds three men, not one. They accept Abraham's hospitality together, and together they prophesy the birth of Isaac. The fearsome God recedes as a different aspect of God's self is revealed, a God who offers a covenant of life and prosperity to the people through Abraham, and the people glimpse grace.

Humanity's encounter with the Trinity expanded with the birth of Jesus of Nazareth, the incarnation of the Second Person of the Trinity, who came to live among us. Jesus routinely spoke about the Father in the third person—someone other than himself—and as one who is within him, one with whom he is one (John 17:22). Jesus, the Holy Spirit, and the Creator appear together at the baptism of Jesus (John 1:32–33) and Jesus refers to both the Father and the Spirit in John 14:16–17. John the Baptist refers to all three persons of the Trinity in John 3:34–35. Jesus makes it clear that he understands himself as distinct from the Father and the Holy Spirit, but is deeply connected to them. Jesus sees himself as "one" with the Father and sees the Holy Spirit as a peer, "Helper," sent by the Father to be present in Jesus's name when Jesus returns to the Father (John 14:26).

Jesus describes himself as intimately tied to the Father and to the Spirit—he is one of three, and each of the three plays a distinct and important role in their relationship with humanity. The Creator brings new things into being, the Word helps us know God through his incarnated humanity, and the Spirit lives within us to constantly remind and teach us of the presence of God. Jesus explicitly says that he and the Father are one, and the Spirit continues Jesus's role as the Teacher and Comforter after Jesus returns to the Father, making the Spirit his peer. The three form a single community, working cooperatively through a deep connection to each other.

Scripture is simply not explicit about the nature of the connection between the three persons of the Trinity. As early Christians struggled to reconcile the God they thought they knew through scripture with the God they physically encountered through Jesus and the God they spiritually encountered through the Holy Spirit, they searched, prayed, and argued their way through several explanations. Beginning as early as the second century, Christians proposed various models and metaphors to attempt to define the relationship between the Three. The writings that would ultimately become canonized as the New Testament clearly stated the existence of Father, Son, and Spirit (e.g., Matt 28:19) but remained silent about the relationship among them.

Complicated theological theories of hierarchy, adoption, and generation initially focused on the relationship between God and Jesus, and then, ultimately, including their relationship with the Holy Spirit. The debate came to a turning point in the early fourth century with the work of Arius, who proposed a hierarchical arrangement that subordinated Jesus to God the Father, saying that Jesus was a creation of God the Father and therefore a creature. Alexander, the bishop of Alexandria, responded to Arius by drawing on the thought of Origen, arguing that Jesus is coeternal with God the Father, and therefore not a creature. The debate between the two became sufficiently heated that it drew the attention of the Roman Empire. Emperor Constantine, through some combination of his mother's influence, a miraculous vision, and political expediency, chose to make Christianity legal in the early fourth century. By the end of the century, the empire had made Christianity the official religion to use it as a unifying influence and to defuse it as a destabilizing one. Encouraged by the political power of Rome to resolve their differences, the bishops of the large churches of the day came together in a series of councils at Antioch, Nicaea, and Constantinople to debate the issue of the Trinity. The direct participation of Constantine added a dimension of political authority to the conclusions reached at Nicaea, but, ultimately, it was the work of Athanasius of Alexandria and of the Cappadocian Fathers that provided the theological underpinnings for the understanding of Trinity that has been held as doctrine since that time. The Council of Constantinople clarified and confirmed the idea initially stated in Nicaea that God is of one substance (*ousia*) and three persons (*hypostases*).[1] One God, three individuals. Three who are equal in one continual unity.

This lengthy history lesson is necessary to appreciate how difficult it has been for humanity to embrace the idea that it is the very nature of God to exist in relationship. God exists as a unique interactive relationship between three distinct but inseparable persons who share a single substance and power. God is three and God is one simultaneously in a cooperative relationship that shares everything.

Theologians wrestled with this concept because it is so different from any example that we see in the natural world and it is so central to imagining who God really is. The natural world is full

1. This historical discussion has relied heavily on the Introduction in Rusch, *The Trinitarian Controversy*.

of examples of organisms—lichen, coral, fish—that are discrete individuals that gather together to form intimately interconnected "communities" for the good of the whole. However, those "communities" are not individuals themselves—they are always groups of individuals. The mystery of the Trinity is that God is simultaneously one and three. They are individuals and wholly complete unto themselves and are also a single entity that is wholly complete.

Because they are one, the wishes and characteristics of one Person of the Trinity apply equally to all three persons of the Trinity. The deep integration of the persons of the Trinity is sometimes described by the Greek word *perichoresis,* which many define using words like interpenetration or complete commingling. The idea is that the persons of the Trinity are still individuals, but are so completely immersed in one another, through love, that they are one. My favorite image of *perichoresis* is that of a circle dance where the dancing individuals whirl and swing in such rhythm and unity that it seems as if they are a single living entity. Creator, Redeemer, and Sustainer joined together in a dance of love—separate, but together.

Remember to think of these things in the present tense, not as something that happened long ago. The Creator is not simply the one who created, but the One who is creating. The Redeemer is redeeming and the Sustainer is sustaining. Many of us talk about the "living God" and are then terribly surprised when God shows up tangibly in our lives through the grace of another person or through the Holy Spirit. The dance of the Trinity is real and vital, and grasping that concept changes everything.

The concept of the Trinity is much more than a bit of Christian theological trivia. The incarnation, the crucifixion, and the resurrection all take on new meaning when seen through the lens of the Trinity. In fact, it may be the most important single concept to appreciate in Christianity. The understanding that community—three together as one—is essential to the nature of God informs and enlightens practically every aspect of being a Christian person.

God loves us because it is the very nature of God to love.

God wants us to love God because it is the very nature of God to love.

God wants us to love each other because it is the very nature of God to love.

Here are some key concepts important to appreciating the Trinity:

- God is three and one at the same time and always.
- The persons of the Trinity are individuals connected by an inseparable bond of love.
- The persons of the Trinity are equal.
- The persons of the Trinity share all knowledge and features.
- The persons of the Trinity are always engaged in the beautiful dance of perichoresis.
- The persons of the Trinity are always in community.

Questions for Reflection

1. Do you have an example or image that helps you understand the Trinity? Do you have images or understandings of the Trinity you may need to rethink?

2. Is God the Father the most important person of the Trinity?

3. Is it important that the dominant political power of the time participated in reaching the current theological understanding of the Trinity?

4. What does it mean when we say God loves us? When we say we love God?

5. Why is the concept of the Trinity important in understanding community?

2

The Nature of Humanity

FOR AS LONG AS scripture has existed, people have struggled with how scripture should be interpreted. Is the Genesis story to be interpreted literally? Many Christian readers see God as Trinity in the first verses of the first book of the Bible, Genesis. If we accept those verses as a source of insight into the nature of God, do we also need to accept the remainder of the story as fact? Did the three persons of the Trinity hover over the void and create everything in six days, or is the creation story an illustration or an allegory to help us grasp the idea that creation flowed from God? Regardless of how we approach it, the story itself is important in this context because it informs us about the nature of humanity. Whether we choose to read Genesis as literal facts or as a beautiful story through which to learn, the story of creation sheds light on who we are.

The story of the creation of humanity in Genesis 1 begins with a subtle reinforcement of God as Trinity. In verse 26, God speaks in the plural, saying, "Let us make humanity in our image," rather than "I will make humanity in my image." We can imagine the persons of the Trinity together as they create people who resemble them.

The next verse further amplifies the resemblance between God and humanity. Verse 27 includes three important statements about God's creation of humanity. The first of these is the act of creation itself: this single verse states three times that God created humanity. This repetition emphasizes God's repeated declarations that creation is good. The second critical statement is that humanity is created in the divine image. Humanity is not God, but humanity reflects God, including the parts of God that are uniquely God-like. The final critical statement is that God created them male and female, confirming that God's image includes both genders.

The creation story continues with God instructing humanity to be fertile, to care for the animals, and to receive plants to eat. God creates humanity in God's image so that humanity might be responsible for all animal life. At the conclusion of the story, God reviewed all of creation and deemed it very good. Thus blessed, humanity begins life in God's creation.

Genesis tells the creation story from two perspectives. The version in chapter 2 provides insights and observations different from those described in chapter 1. Chapter 2 gives a more intimate accounting of the creation of humanity, telling us that God formed the first human out of the "topsoil of the fertile land" and blew the breath of life into his nostrils. God provided for the human by planting a beautiful garden, full of edible fruit, to be his home. The human is well taken care of. Then, in verse 18, God makes a startling observation—it is not good for the human to be alone. The scripture does not disclose how God knew this—was the human sad, or lonely, or depressed? We are only told that for the first time in the creation story, God says something in creation is "not good"—the human is alone.

Looking at the stories together provides an insight. The human is made in God's image, yet is not in community. The human is an individual, a single person, and is alone. God has lavishly provided for the human's environment and nutrition, but at this point in the story, God has not yet provided for a fundamental need that flows from the image of God—someone to love.

The Genesis story proceeds with what at first glance appears to be a bit of trial and error on God's part. God creates animals to keep the human company and gives the human the job of naming them. It is as if God is a young mother whose baby is fussing for no obvious reason, and she is running through all the possibilities to make the baby feel better. The baby is warm, well fed, seems to have a clean diaper—and still the baby fusses. The helper who is perfect for the human is nowhere to be found.

God then chooses to create another human out of the flesh and bone of the first one. The first human is delighted, and human community is formed. Creation is balanced, as the humans love each other and God in a beautiful garden that meets all of their needs.

It's tempting to push ahead to Genesis 3 with a gruff, "Well that didn't last, did it?" but doing so would miss some important points. It is noteworthy that the first thing that God points out as "not good" is the lack of community, not original sin! God sees that the human needs another human for creation to be "good" as God intended.

Reflecting further on chapter 2, God's "trial and error" turns out to be instruction. From the very beginning of life, the human feels a fundamental need that is only fulfilled through a relationship with another person. That need is not fulfilled by time spent with other creatures and it is not fulfilled by work. Apparently, it is not even fulfilled by a relationship with God! It is only satisfied by a relationship with another human. The human comes to learn, through lived experience, that he needs to be in relationship with God and another human to be fulfilled.

This observation leads us to the important conclusion that, because humanity is created in the image of God and the fundamental nature of God includes being in community, the need for community is part of the fundamental nature of humanity. Community is not simply pleasant or efficient; it is a central part of who we are. Because we reflect the nature of God, we reflect the fundamental identity of God as three-in-one.

And, as if that were not enough, the identification of humanity's need for community leads us to an even deeper observation: humans achieve their purpose in life through community. As the first human learned through God's "trial and error," fulfillment does not come from work alone or through isolated relationships with God and creation. The human is complete when in community with God and other humans. Community allows the human to consider the wants and needs of the other. The human grows by looking outside of the human's self, through loving and giving, and through doing work with the purpose of contributing to the well-being of another or being obedient to God. The role of the human becomes growth through the love of God and the love of others—a very positive life mission when contrasted with the more traditional view of a life mission of atoning for eating forbidden fruit. Humanity was created to be encircled in God's love and to encircle others in that love. God's grace empowers the forgiven to stand tall to be hugged.

On the night of his betrayal, Jesus prayed a beautiful prayer that affirms this observation. In John 17, Jesus prays for his disciples and for those who come to believe in him through their word, which encompasses everyone who learns of Jesus through the gospels written by the disciples. He prays that they (and we) will become one with him and one with each other, just as he and the Father are one. Jesus refers to the bond of love that connects the First Person of the Trinity with the Second and then prays that we may be connected to him and to each other in exactly the same way. In verse 23, he says, "I'm in them and you are in me so that they will be made perfectly one." It is through the sharing of that connection of love between Jesus and the Father that unity is achieved among humans.

Combining these threads, we may glimpse the bigger picture. Humanity is created by God, in the image of God, who breathes the breath of life into each person. Therefore, each person is a unique individual who reflects an inherent need for community with God and others because community is central to the very being of God. As each individual lives into this need by fostering bonds of community through loving and serving others, they live into Jesus's prayer for unity with God and others. As the individual grows and enters into justifying grace—the choice of a committed relationship with Jesus through the Holy Spirit—that unity grows and is strengthened. Seeing the meaning of human life in this way helps us appreciate the brilliance of God's creative energy. God creates each of us as individuals and then sets us on unique and diverse adventures. Some of us live happy lives and some of us lead difficult lives, but all of us live lives in the presence of God and others. Our unique experiences shape us into who we are, and God's great gift of life and salvation allows each of our individual selves to be shared with God-self and other created individuals.

And then, at the end of earthly life, when the individual exhales for the last time, God receives that unique individual into the full unity that Jesus prays for us to join. As created, beloved individuals, we are welcomed into the unity of the Trinity and the communion of saints. It is hard to imagine anything more wonderful and amazing. It is as if the completeness of creation grows infinitely through God's creative force. It is complete at this instant, and it will be complete in a new way in every moment hereafter through the addition of the experiences and individuality of each of God's children.

Here are some key concepts in appreciating humanity as created in God's image:

- God created humanity.

- God created humanity in God's image.

- Community is an integral part of God's image.

- God observed that it was "not good" that the first human was alone.

- Work, animals, and even being alone with God did not satisfy the human need for community.

- Community allows humans to focus outside of themselves, which helps them grow in love.

- The prayer of Jesus is that humanity should be one with him and each other as he is one with God the Father.

- The purpose of human life can be imagined as the growth and development of a unique and individual expression of love for God and others, which ultimately becomes part of the unity of God and others for eternity.

Questions for Reflection

1. Why did God wait to create the human's companion?

2. Does it feel unusual to think about the creation story without focusing on the apple and the snake?

3. Do you agree that community is critical to human happiness?

4. How does eternal unity with God and with others fit into your understanding of "heaven" or the afterlife?

5. Can people be happy when focusing exclusively on themselves?

3

The Story of Grace

GOD DID NOT CREATE humanity and then simply set it on its way to see what might happen. From the very beginning of the Bible, God is in relationship with people, providing blessings of guidance and resources for their benefit. Those blessings may be called God's "grace," which is the "undeserved, unmerited, and loving action of God in human existence through the ever-present Holy Spirit."[1] Looking through scripture chronologically reveals that the ways that God's grace typically flows into the world—the "means" of grace—change as the story of God and humanity develops.

In the creation story in Genesis 2, God creates a beautiful garden, a landscape of grace, filled with everything the human needs and then joins them, physically, in community. The story describes God as a nurturing parent, talking with the humans and attending to their needs. Verse 15 says that God "settled him in" the garden and gave him a way to contribute to his community and be productive.

In Genesis 3, the story shifts when the humans choose to do something that God has told them not to. Many of us who know the story of the apple and the snake have been taught to describe

1. *The Book of Discipline of The United Methodist Church 2012,* ¶102.

that moment as the "original sin"—the moment when Eve (it is clearly the woman's fault) messed up everything by listening to the snake, eating the apple, and sharing it with Adam, who was drawn in by her wiles in a moment of weakness (clearly a man would never make a choice like that on his own!). God confronts them, curses them, and expels them from God's presence to struggle in the cold, cruel world. Humanity shows its true colors as totally depraved and grovels aimlessly in the muck until God, the Angry Father, takes out his rage on Jesus, the Innocent Son, several thousand years later.

But as prevalent as that interpretation of the story is, it is not the only possible interpretation. Because humanity is created in the image of God, we have the ability to make choices. The Creator created us that way, and declared creation "supremely good." As the humans grew, they made a choice that was contrary to God's will. God explained that their choice had consequences—it took them away from the paradise that God desired for them. God clothed them for the journey, and they set out to find their way.

From that perspective, one can read the entire Bible as the story of humanity's journey through time with God, told through the mediums of narrative, history, poetry, and drama. We can watch humanity grow and change, evolving from nomadic family groups into nations, and, as a result, watch humanity's perception of God grow and change from patriarch to warlord to sovereign king. The recurring theme is one of covenant, in which God repeatedly stepped into the lives of the people, offering them relationship. In story after story, God provided for humans, asking only for their love in return. This pattern echoed the earliest promises God spoke to Abram in Genesis 12—I will bless you so that you might be a blessing to others. God asked nothing in return other than to be loved by them. In Genesis 17, God offered Abraham and his descendants a most wonderful relationship—I will be your God and you will be my people. Time and time again, God called people back to God, blessing them that they might bless each other, and that they might love God.

In the stories of the Old Testament, God interacts with the people through intermediaries chosen by God. Those intermediaries ranged from Moses to Jeremiah and filled a variety of roles. Some of the intermediaries were leaders who heard directly from God regarding actions to be taken on God's behalf. In Exodus 3 and 4, Moses, the man chosen by God to lead the Israelites out of Egypt, engaged in an extended argument with God regarding whether he was the right person to confront Pharaoh and to lead the people out of slavery. Scripture describes the encounter as Moses literally arguing with a voice emanating from a burning bush—quite an intense confrontation! Moses met God directly many times to receive instruction and to intercede on behalf of the people when they lost hope and faith.

As the story of God's people continued, their leaders were counseled or confronted by prophets, people who heard instruction from God, usually in the form of a call to repentance and a return to the ways God had provided for the people. Over time, the role of the people changed: from listening directly to the voice of God, to adhering to the rules provided by God, and then to adhering to the volumes of rules added by religious leaders. Humanity, because of its ability to choose for itself, often took a path away from God. In a pattern that recurs throughout the Old Testament, the people chose to stray from God's will in favor of their own desires, and poor choices often led to disastrous consequences.

And in the midst of a very difficult time for the people, God chose to come to them as Jesus of Nazareth. The lands of the Jewish people had been overrun by the Roman Empire, and what was left of the local political government was completely subservient to the occupying Romans. The religious leadership of the time seemed focused on observing the minutiae of every rule, often to the detriment of the people themselves. Jesus, born in Bethlehem because his family had been required by the occupying Romans to travel to his father's familial home city to register for taxation, entered the world as a poor Palestinian Jew. Jesus grew up in Nazareth, working at the side of his father, the carpenter, in a small fishing village. Around the age of thirty, Jesus began an itinerant ministry, living simply and preaching love and compassion for the poor. He confronted the religious leadership, teaching that they had totally missed the point of scripture by emphasizing rule-keeping over love of neighbor. He lived in a God-focused manner, praying often and lavishing his time and energy on the poor and marginalized. He lived in the light of God's love and grace.

The greatest example of God's grace toward humanity comes in the death and resurrection of Jesus, who taught us that the gift of life in God's grace transcends our simple earthly life. In John 17, Jesus prays for all of humanity—for everyone who knows him through the words of his disciples—to become one with him and one with each other. Jesus shows us the incredible power of that unity within the love of the Trinity by enduring the worst that the world had to offer—betrayal, subterfuge, injustice, torture, and death—only to return to physical life to demonstrate that God's love conquers all that evil can muster against it. The resurrection of Jesus was not some amazing magic trick to impress us all. Exactly like the rest of Jesus's life, his resurrection is a tangible example of a human life lived in concert with God's grace. He is the first of humanity to physically demonstrate that human death does not end humanity's unity with God. Jesus shows us, in his journey through death to resurrection, that God's grace flows to us and within us always, and that God's grace grants us the opportunity to join in the life of God and the life of humanity for all time.

Through the life, death, and resurrection of Jesus, God gave humanity a living example of a human life lived in concert with God's grace. The life of Jesus showed what it means to be God-centered and deeply focused on the love of God and others. His life was a wonderful example of *kenosis*, the selfless giving of one's energy and resources, and of the need for rest in God's grace to replenish those resources to be given again.[2] Jesus demonstrated how to live in the flow of God's grace in normal, everyday life. His life revealed that the gift of life through God's grace is without limits, and that God's love triumphs over evil without exception.

2. For a detailed discussion of this topic, please see Duggins, *Simple Harmony*, chapter 6.

A careful examination of Jesus's life of grace reveals several specific human ways in which he sought to interact with God and God's grace. These particular activities and behaviors—including prayer, spending time in scripture, and others—ultimately become known as the "instituted" means of grace, because Jesus instituted or established them by routinely using them to encounter God's grace. Focusing on Jesus's behavior in the gospels, we can identify the practices that Jesus typically employed to intentionally connect with God.

Jesus prayed often. Scripture describes three of the prayers of Jesus in detail, particularly the prayer that Jesus taught the disciples when they asked him to teach them to pray. Appearing in Matthew 6 and Luke 11, the prayer is simple and profound. Jesus begins with words of praise for the Father, followed by an expression of his desire that the will of God be fully embraced on earth. He asks for the nourishment he will need for this day, for forgiveness of sin, and for protection against temptations that might lead him away from God's will. In this humble little prayer, Jesus praises God and asks for God's grace to fulfill his basic needs and to align his personal will with the will of God. It is almost as if Jesus asks the Father to return with him to the joy and simplicity of the garden of Eden.

Jesus's prayers in another garden, the Garden of Gethsemane, also reflect this desire for the alignment of his will with God's. In Matthew 26, Jesus is sad and anxious as he anticipates his arrest and trial, and he prays for an alternative to the ordeal that he sees as God's will. He concludes that prayer, however, with a request that his will be the same as the Father's—a prayer for God's grace to help Jesus be obedient.

On the night of his betrayal, Jesus spoke with God the Father directly and conversationally through prayer (see John 17). Jesus asked the Father to complete the work that had been begun by the Father by glorifying Jesus during his ministry, but then he shifted the emphasis of his prayer to the protection of his disciples, and he asked that God would make them holy through the truth. He asked that God make them one with each other and with Jesus, as the Father and Jesus are one, that they might know eternal life through knowing the Father and the Christ. He prayed for the ultimate grace—that humanity, through the love of Jesus, would enter into an eternal unity with God and each other.

In addition to these particular prayers through which we are able to see Jesus's appeals for God's grace, there are many more examples of Jesus withdrawing to pray scattered throughout the gospels. Jesus retreated when he heard about the murder of John the Baptist and he was away in prayer before he fed the five thousand and before he walked on the Sea of Galilee to meet the disciples. He prayed before selecting the disciples. Prayer—and perhaps withdrawn prayer, in particular—was a vital link between Father and Son, a normal and recurring way that Jesus experienced the Father's grace.

Jesus engaged in the spiritual practice of fasting. After his baptism by John the Baptist described in Luke 4, Jesus withdraws into the desert wilderness to fast and to pray. During that time, the devil tempted Jesus to use his ability to make choices contrary to God's will to grasp resources, wealth, and power. In response to each temptation, Jesus quoted from scripture, indicating that he understood his path in life in part as the result of searching and studying scripture. In one case, the devil tries to twist scripture to pull Jesus in the wrong direction, and Jesus responds with another scripture that correctly interpreted God's will for him. Jesus did not simply "proof-text" as the devil did, pulling a passage out of context to support an argument of his own making, but rather, Jesus used scripture to inform and guide his understanding of God's desires for him and to support living in a particular way.

This understanding of scripture as a means for God to speak into Jesus's life is very clear in the next story found in Luke 4. Jesus returned from the desert and began to teach. He attended synagogue on the Sabbath in Nazareth as he usually did, and stood to read scripture. He was given the scroll of the writings of the prophet Isaiah, and turned to the passage we now identify as Isaiah 61:1–2a:

The Lord God's spirit is upon me,
because the Lord has anointed me.
He has sent me
to bring good news to the poor,
to bind up the brokenhearted,
to proclaim release for captives,
and liberation for prisoners,
to proclaim the year of the Lord's favor
and a day of vindication for our God.

Jesus then told the captivated congregation that the scripture had been fulfilled that day in their hearing, claiming that role as his own. Jesus turned to scripture to describe his role in life rather than crafting a mission statement of his own. Scripture informed him as he sought to give words to the call and charge that he felt in his life.

Luke 4 also gives insight into two other spiritual practices Jesus followed in order to connect with God. The story of his time in the wilderness describes him fasting, which is the practice of foregoing something familiar in order to draw one's attention to God. It is likely that Jesus abstained from eating, as the devil's first temptation of Jesus had to do with food. The story of the reading in the synagogue mentions that Jesus went to the synagogue on the Sabbath as he normally did, indicating that participation in Sabbath worship was a regular part of Jesus's life.

Conversations can also be a conduit of God's grace. Throughout the gospels, Jesus discussed the meaning of scripture with a variety of people. He often clashed with the Pharisees over the interpretation of Sabbath rules, and he also debated the relative importance of commandments and the priority of love over rule-keeping. These discussions are interwoven into his teachings, along with his parables and his direct teachings, as one of the ways to go deeper into the meaning of living as God's people. Jesus experienced God's grace through scripture as he struggled alongside other believers to uncover faithful interpretations of particular passages through debate and discussion.

Just as Jesus leaned into the story of grace to connect with God through study and prayer, Jesus also reshaped a familiar Jewish religious ritual as a means for his followers to "remember" and draw closer to him. Luke 22 recounts the Passover meal that Jesus celebrated with his close followers on the night of his betrayal and arrest. The Passover meal was a familiar ritual among the Jewish people that recalled the protection of the Jewish firstborn from the final plague in Egypt and the Hebrew slaves' exodus from bondage. Jesus took the bread and wine served at the Passover meal and asked those present to think of him as they ate and drank these familiar foods at this and every meal. He described the bread as his broken body and the wine as his spilled blood, redefining the covenant between God and humanity through his gift of death and resurrection. The Lord's Supper, as this sacrament would become known, recounts the life of Jesus and his ongoing presence in the daily life of humanity.

Considering these activities together, we can identify the regular means through which God's grace flowed through the life of Jesus: prayer, studying scripture, fasting, worship, discussions with other believers, and the Lord's Supper. Of course, God's grace entered Jesus's life in other ways too, but these represent the ordinary, established ways that God interacts with people. Scripture shows us that God continually reaches into the lives of people through grace, so it makes good sense that normal, recurring pathways would be established for this. If every encounter with God was seen to be unusual or miraculous, the entire idea of a desire by God to be part of every human life would be nonsense. God established these "means of grace" to be part of daily life, or predictable ways to encounter and interact with God.

The concept of the means of grace was very important to John Wesley and appears throughout his teaching in a variety of combinations. In his sermon "The Means of Grace," Wesley describes the means of grace as "outward signs, words, or actions" established by God to be the most common ways that God conveys grace to people. He speaks of the means of grace as "ordinances"— outward means ordained by Christ for conveying grace into the hearts of people. In that sermon, Wesley focuses on prayer, scripture, and the Lord's Supper, and he goes to great lengths to explain that the power of the means of grace is not in the acts themselves, but rather lies in the mutual desire for connection between God and humanity. He expands his discussion of the means of grace in Question 48 of the "Large Minutes," a statement of doctrine and discipline in the form of questions and answers that arose out of Methodist Conferences held in the second half of the eighteenth century. The "Large Minutes" addresses a question regarding the evaluation of others, and Wesley goes into some detail regarding the means of grace. He provides a listing of what he describes as the "instituted" means of grace, meaning those that were established directly through the example of Jesus. They include prayer, searching scripture, the Lord's Supper, fasting, and Christian conferencing.

In his "Large Minutes" response, Wesley goes on to describe "prudential" means of grace, or activities and actions that lead to interactions with God's grace that are not directly attributable to examples from the life of Jesus. Used in this context, the term *prudential* is defined as flowing from prudence, or the reasonable and rational use of judgment. Wesley lists a variety of actions and ideas as prudential means of grace, including rules of life, temperance, moderation, and faithfulness. The understanding of prudential means of grace has grown to include activities such as Wesleyan class and band meetings, love feasts, and covenant renewal services. The concept of prudential means of grace invites humanity to openly seek ways to routinely encounter God's grace, and to allow the understanding of those means to change over time. This flexibility in both practice and doctrine reflects the active nature of God as creator, allowing the means of grace to grow and change as creation grows and changes.

Here are some key concepts in appreciating God's grace and the ways it enters the world:

- Grace is the "undeserved, unmerited and loving action of God in human existence through the ever-present Holy Spirit."

- God has brought grace into the lives of humanity from the moment of creation, and the reliable ways that God delivers such grace into human lives are called "the means of grace."

- The concept of the "means of grace" is important in Wesleyan theology.

- Jesus lived a life deeply connected to God's grace.

- The death and resurrection of Jesus connects us to the reality that the flow of God's grace does not end with human death.

- Jesus showed humanity a variety of ways to encounter God's grace in the course of daily life. These include prayer, carefully studying scripture, fasting, worship, discussions with other believers, and the Lord's Supper. These practices later became known as the "instituted means of grace" because Jesus practiced them.

- In addition to the "instituted" means of grace, there are "prudential" or common-sense means of grace that Jesus did not directly institute.

- The prudential means of grace change as people change. The instituted means of grace are consistently available through time.

Questions for Reflection

1. Does it make sense to you that some of the ordinary ways that God's grace flows into the lives of people change over time and that some do not change?

2. How does viewing Genesis 3 as the story of humanity setting out to find its way rather than shredding its relationship with God through sin affect your image of God?

3. In the timeline of the Old Testament, people move from talking directly to God, to talking to God through prophets, to simply obeying rules set forth by God and people, only then to encounter God-with-us in the person of Jesus. How does this personal encounter with God shift the flow of grace in the lives of the people?

4. Do you believe that the life of Jesus is an example to live by? What forces make that difficult?

5. Does the concept of "ordinary, established" ways for God's grace to flow into the lives of people make sense to you?

4

Community Is a Means of Grace

I BELIEVE THAT COMMUNITY itself is a prudential means of grace. Our Creator lives in a constant state of life-giving community, thriving through an inseparable bond between Father, Son, and Spirit. Our Creator made us in the Creator's image, so we, ourselves, long for the same kind of community connection, and it is the prayer of the Redeemer that we experience that kind of community with each other and with the Creator. Through learning to love each other in communities, we live into our nature as the reflection of the image of God, fulfilling the desire of God, which draws us closer to God.

It is clear that John Wesley included particular forms of community in his understanding of the means of grace. He specifically mentioned class meetings, bands, and select societies as Methodist forms of accountability groups that supported people in their positive response to God's grace.[1] He taught that communal support of each other was essential to living and growing in response to God's grace, authorizing a hymnic prayer on the topic written by his brother Charles for use in society meetings:

1. Maddox, *Responsible Grace*, 212.

25

Help us to help each other, Lord,
  Each other's cross to bear;
Let each his friendly aid afford,
  And feel his brother's care.

Help us to build each other up,
  Our little stock improve;
Increase our faith, confirm our hope,
  And perfect us in love.[2]

Wesley saw Christian accountability and the accompanying mutual support as critical components to Christian growth and deepening responsiveness to God's grace. In this way, being in community supported growth in holiness.

Wesley also included "Christian conference" as an instituted means of grace in the "Large Minutes." He had a particular type of communal interaction in mind when he used that term: an honest, direct discussion, about one hour in length, beginning and ending in prayer, and intended to help each participant grow in holiness.[3] This type of conversation echoes the function of a class meeting, but might occur outside of that context.

Wesley emphasized the importance of conversation among believers as a way to encourage and sharpen individual responses to God's grace. In his sermon "The First Fruits of the Spirit," he describes "holiness of conversation" as a characteristic of people who are part of the body of Christ, and as a means "meet to minister grace to the hearers."[4] He sees discussion as a way for people to grow and learn and as a way for more mature Christians to share their experience with those who are earlier in their walk towards holiness. In "The Cure of Evil Speaking," Wesley builds a strong argument for uplifting speech and against destructive speech on the

---

2. "A Prayer for Persons Joined in Fellowship," stanzas 3 and 4; quoted in ibid., 210.

3. Kevin Watson, "Holy Conferencing: What Did Wesley Mean? (Part 2)," *Vital Piety* (blog), July 18, 2013, https://vitalpiety.com/2013/07/18/holy-conferencing-what-did-wesley-mean-part-2.

4. Wesley, "The First Fruits of the Spirit," I.5.

basis of Matthew 18:15–17.[5] He outlines a biblical pattern for the direction and correction of those who are not living as they should, using private speech, small groups, and the gathered society as the tools for instruction and direction. Wesley sees conversation in this context, in both public and private forms, as a means of grace.

Wesley also makes a strong argument for a particular type of community, the class meeting, as a prudential means of grace. In "A Plain Account of the People Called Methodists," he says this about the impact of class meetings:

> It can scarce be conceived what advantages have been reaped from this little prudential regulation. Many now happily experienced that Christian fellowship of which they had not so much as an idea before. They began to "bear one another's burdens," and "naturally" to "care for each other." As they had daily a more intimate acquaintance with, so they had a more endeared affection for each other. And "speaking the truth in love, they grew up into him in all things which is the head, even Christ; from whom the whole body, fitly joined together, and compacted by that which every joint supplied, according to the effectual working in the measure of every part, increased unto the edifying itself in love."[6]

The class meeting is a particular type of community, structured along a particular set of rules and practices, with the specific intent of providing a forum for accountability and spiritual growth. As Wesley mentions, the class meeting engenders the growth of friendship and then love among its participants, who develop an intimate bond of trust and connection over time. His use of the body of Christ language implies that he sees the class meeting community growing into an organic whole that includes each of the members of the community and Christ.

---

5. Wesley, "The Cure of Evil Speaking."

6. Wesley, "A Plain Account of the People Called Methodists," in Wesley, *Works*, 9:262.

Wesley also includes other specifically Methodist forms of gatherings in his listings of the prudential means of grace.[7] He argues that "love feasts," gatherings during which unconsecrated bread and water are shared among the participants, "nourish" people through the telling and hearing of personal testimonies. "Watch Night" and "Covenant Renewal" services provided the participants with periodic opportunities to reflect on their commitment to Christian life and on remaining instances of sin within their lives. Within Methodism, these "Watch Night" and "Covenant Renewal" gatherings eventually evolved into annual reflections on God's grace typically held around New Year's Day.

To summarize, it is very clear that Wesley appreciated the power of particular manifestations of community as a means of grace. He counted Christian conferencing among the means of grace particularly instituted by Jesus, and taught broadly about supporting each other in Christian growth through discussion, caring for one another, and instruction. He gathered his followers into communities designed to help them grow in faith and to avoid temptation. It seems that Wesley would look to the *intent* of the community to assess whether the community could act as a means of grace.

If community—a group of people gathered together under some unifying principle or for some particular purpose—can in fact be a means of grace, one must ask whether it is *always* a means of grace or whether it is *potentially* a means of grace. For me, this question revolves around Wesley's question of intent—do the members of the community intend to grow in love with each other? Do they intend to seek God? In the Wesleyan class meeting, considered by Wesley to be a means of grace, the participants gather under the supervision of the larger Methodist society with particular directions and questions to explore together. Does this standard imply that the quilting guild at the church is not a means of grace, but the Sunday school class is?

It seems obvious that some particular communities are not means of grace—dog fighting clubs come to mind—so, barring

7. Maddox, *Responsible Grace*, 209–11.

groups gathered around evil intent, I would propose that every other community has the potential to be a means of grace. Recognizing that the potential is realized through the intent and responsiveness of the group, particularly in the light of Matthew 18:20—"For where two or three are gathered in my name, I'm there with them"—it becomes clear that the key is "in my name." Is the community gathered in the name of Christ, or are they willing to consider and acknowledge the presence of Christ among them? If the answer is yes, or even maybe, God can use that community to pour grace into the lives of the participants.

In this day and age, it seems vitally important to be gentle and open with the definition of "in my name." If we insist on labeling groups in an explicitly Christian manner—calling the gymnastics group in the church gym "Jumping for Jesus"—we might inadvertently exclude people who are interested in joining a group of people who enjoy gymnastics but are repelled by their perceptions of what Christianity is. By calling the group something neutral like "the Gymnastics Group," we offer the opportunity to become part of a caring community to everyone, which, in turn, allows the interaction of Christians and non-Christians in a positive environment.

"Bait and switch!" you scream at the top of your lungs. Absolutely not. Bait-and-switch tactics are wrong and are part of the tradition that makes many people wary of any interaction with organized religion at all.

We live in a media-filled world that is continually telling stories. Unfortunately, this encourages using stereotypes as shortcuts to make storytelling easier. As a result, negative stereotypes about Christians and Christianity are continually reinforced and come to form the basis upon which many people shape their ideas about who Christians are. For example, imagine that some small fundamentalist Christian church organizes a protest at the funeral of a gay person who was a public figure in order to proclaim their position against same-gender marriage. Because the very idea of protesting at a funeral is so repulsive, it makes good news fodder. The journalist has ninety seconds to tell the story under the video images, so she really does not have time to qualify the fact that the options and tactics of this little group do not represent main-line Christianity as a whole—she just refers to them as a Christian group while the video shows them shouting and condemning the family who has gathered to mourn the loss of a loved one. The viewers, unavoidably, form negative impressions of Christianity as a whole.

A number of years ago, I attended the Parliament of World Religions in Melbourne, Australia. An atheist group was protesting the conference because they were not allowed to participate, and, on a whim, I sat down with one of the protesters to hear her story. She was in her middle sixties and was quite vocal and energetic. She explained the reason that she was protesting to me, and then she launched into a pretty vehement attack on all the stupid Christians who think everyone is going to hell—especially the gay people and the atheists and those who believe in evolution. I listened, and then replied, "Well, I am a Christian, I believe in evolution and I have gay friends and support the ordination of gay people and I believe God is working very hard to invite everyone to be loved." She looked at me with a shocked look, was silent for a couple seconds, and then sputtered, "Well, you are just not a real Christian!"

Community offers the chance to confront those stereotypes in a positive, person-to-person manner. There is a saying attributed to St. Francis of Assisi that goes, "Preach the Gospel at all times. Use words if necessary." That concept—living a life that follows the example of Jesus in the presence of people who are part of your community but who have not encountered "non-stereotype" Christians—sits at the heart of community as a means of grace, especially as a means of prevenient grace, which is God's grace in a person's life before a relationship with Christ. Imagine Christians, joined with others in communities that are important to people of this day and age, living as followers of Christ ready to be the hands and feet of Christ in the lives of those who do not yet know how to express their "spiritual but not religious" feelings. Christians sharing their stories and experiences with people who are truly their friends, not to push them into conversion or membership, but because, as a friend, they want to share what is important to them. Christian people who model love and inclusion in community. Christians who are willing to help others see the presence of Christ in their midst.

The closing scenes of the musical *Les Misérables* revolve around the death of the aged protagonist, Jean Valjean. Finally at peace after a lifelong struggle for mercy and justice, Valjean, with the spirits of Fantine and Eponine, whom he loved and each of whom helped shape Valjean into a figure of grace, reminds us of "the truth that once was spoken: to love another person is to see the face of God."

This is community as a means of grace.

Questions for Reflection

1. Does it make sense to you that God's grace might flow into someone's life through community?

2. Are there communities that are unlikely to be conduits of God's grace? What are their characteristics?

3. Is it wrong to form relationships with the express intent of converting a person to Christianity?

4. Does the media stereotype of Christianity affect your ability to invite people into a Christian relationship? Does it affect your ability to call yourself Christian?

5. Does something have to be called Christian to be Christian?

5

Forming Communities Today

POPULAR MEMORY RECALLS A time when practically everyone in a community attended church on Sunday morning. People then would ask which denomination a person belonged to, rather than if they belonged. Sunday school classes were hubs of friendships, Vacation Bible School was a highlight of the summer, and Friday fish fries brought the whole neighborhood to the Catholic church. Churches often developed a special fundraiser that emerged from the church kitchen—homemade noodles, steak dinners, fried chicken, baked pies, spaghetti dinners—and the whole neighborhood looked forward to them. Women worked in the neighborhood, children went to youth groups, and men did community relief work—all through church-based organizations.

And then things changed. The television made it unnecessary to seek entertainment outside of the home. Young people rebelled against rules and societal and cultural restrictions on behavior. Family structures shifted as divorce rates grew and as two-wage-earner families became common. Programmed activities for children became more popular, squeezing into times that had been previously dedicated to church activities. More recently, the personal computer and the handheld screen have replaced "friends" and "communities" in a totally unprecedented way.

According to Gallup, 91 percent of Americans self-identified as Christian in 1950, as compared to 70 percent today.[1] Actual church attendance is much harder to track, but an interesting study done by Tobin Grant, a political science professor at Southern Illinois University, compares more than four hundred survey results over the past sixty years to create a religiosity index.[2] "Religiosity" is a sociological term for the quality of being religious or pious, so in layman's terms, the index seeks to measure whether people are religious. The index reveals a huge decline in "being religious" from 1952 to 2013.

In less than two generations, the church yielded the focus of neighborhood life. It remains an important focal point for some, but many people have neither the time nor the inclination to foster relationships at the local church. Buildings often sit empty, used once or twice weekly for a dwindling membership.

At the Missional Wisdom Foundation, we observed this phenomenon all over the country, and we began to ask ourselves, If people no longer form community through their church, how do they form community? We began asking questions of and observing groups that we encountered or were engaged in. Over time, answers to our questions began to emerge. We are not social scientists, but the stories we were hearing and our own experiences began to fall together with observable consistency.

The first thing we noticed was, despite the fact that its role as a community hub has diminished, in many places the church continues to play an important role as a center of community. This role varies from church to church and region to region, but church continues to fulfill an important social role for many people. Sunday worship, Sunday school, crafting groups, choirs, and service organizations still fill an important connective function for many people as vital components of their spiritual growth

1. See www.gallup.com/poll/1690/religion.aspx.

2. Tobin Grant, "The Great Decline: 60 Years of Religion in One Graph," *Religion News Service*, January 27, 2014, www.religionnews.com/2014/01/27/great-decline-religion-united-states-one-graph/.

and development. This observation is a critical one as we consider alternative forms of Christian community. We need to be careful to preserve the historic communities within established churches that continue to serve as means of grace. Building new types of Christian community does not require the destruction of the old. It may be necessary to reallocate resources and update priorities, but that can be done within a framework of healthy respect for tradition. There is a temptation to sweep away the old practices and the old congregation because they are no longer attractive to some or because they do not meet some criterion for vitality or financial stability. In many cases that is unnecessary and counterproductive. Embracing the old practices and the old people as a part of developing new forms of community preserves a library of faith and experience, and recognizes the ways in which God has entered the lives of those who came before and those who appreciate and are filled by the old practices. Closed churches that have been transformed into coffee shops make me sad; churches that have incorporated coffee shops into their space and lives give me hope.

During our research, we noticed that many people form community within their workplace. People form friendships with their coworkers and clients that extend outside of the workplace itself. It is not uncommon to find groups of coworkers who socialize together after work or who join each other in fitness or enrichment activities. Many workplaces encourage this interaction through gym membership subsidies or by sponsoring general interest seminars or book clubs after work hours or during lunch breaks.

We also noticed the significance of food and table in community formation. Many of the workplace communities we became aware of revolved around shared meals at lunch or dinner and around after-work "happy hours." The pace of daily life and the increasing number of two-wage-earner families have resulted in a significant increase in dining out, a phenomenon that has led many to join with others while eating. Scanning a restaurant during a weekday evening will often reveal groups of individuals, couples, and families, sharing a meal together.

The restaurant phenomenon has also coincided with a growing interest in the production of fresh, healthy food. Gardening is growing in popularity in a variety of settings. Those concerned with social justice have observed the lack of healthy food options in low-income settings, and community gardens have become a popular response. As neighbors work together to produce food and address the needs of the community, friendships are formed. Also, groups that garden together often realize that many of the food preparation skills taken for granted by older generations have not yet been taught to younger generations, so communities arise around food preparation. Growing, preparing, and sharing food draws people together.

People are also drawn together by their children's school and extracurricular activities. This generation of parents is heavily involved in the daily activities of their children, and the structured organization of children's activities is at an unprecedented high. Club and school sports require an incredible commitment of time and energy by the children and the parents, and children are enrolled in sports from a very young age. The parents of children involved in these types of activities find themselves forming community as they encounter each other at games and practices and as they work together to coordinate travel and fundraising. Additionally, the advent of two-wage-earner families has made after-school enrichment activities very important, providing supervision and instruction while the parents finish the workday. Parents often come together into communities in the coordination and implementation of after-school activities.

Finally, we noticed that people form community through affinity groups, gathering around shared recreational and creative activities as well as shared areas of interest and concern. Participants in 12-step groups gather to support each other in sobriety, while people who are caring for elderly parents gather to share notes and resources. Perhaps as a reaction to the increasingly organized structures around children's sports, we find groups of adults organizing around shared sporting interests like hiking, soccer, and tennis. Many people seem to be looking for groups to share these activities with.

One additional benefit to communities formed around shared creative activities like sewing, quilting, woodworking, pottery, and knitting is that these crafts often have specialized equipment that can be shared or require the investment of a significant amount of time that can be more enjoyable with companions.

The traditional role of the church and of church buildings has been to facilitate the administration of several of the instituted means of grace, including worship, public and private prayer, the Lord's Supper, and the searching of scripture. Specialized forms of gathering such as class meetings, love feasts, and commitment services might also take place on the church grounds. We have noted, however, that many of these "church-based" means of grace no longer seem relevant to the present generation, which has led to a reduction in the number of people who participate in church communities. If one of the primary roles of the church and of church buildings is to promote encounters with the means of grace, how should the church and church buildings change to form communities that are relevant to people today so that those communities might become means of grace? If people form communities around workplace, food, their children's schools and activities, and shared recreational activities, how can the church and the church building change to develop those kinds of communities in a way that helps people see God in their midst?

Questions for Reflection

1. What communities do you belong to?

2. Is it necessary to do away with old communities to create new ones? Why or why not?

3. Why do people become friends at work?

4. Why does community form around children's activities?

5. Can communities formed around work, food, children's activities, and affinity groups be church?

6

Traditional Church as Community

PEOPLE HAVE FORMED COMMUNITY through "church" from early history. The books of Moses refer to people gathering to worship idols and gods and to engage in the rituals of the Jewish people. The books of Samuel document the debate over constructing a temple building and the process of its construction. By the time of Jesus, we read of local temple gatherings in which scripture is read and discussed.

By modern times, cultural norms and rhythms established many of the community-building aspects of church. Sunday morning worship, Wednesday evening dinners and Bible studies, and Friday fish fries became predictable staples of neighborhood and community activity. The centrality of those specific activities as catalysts for community has diminished, but for many they remain important sources of social interaction.

For some, Sunday morning worship remains an important form of community. People gather in an established, often purpose-built location like a sanctuary to engage in group prayer, ritual, singing, and teaching with the intent of worshipping God. They often have particular places within the sanctuary where they sit each week, which can build a sense of comfort and belonging. The people who gather regularly interact with each other before and after the worship service, often around coffee and snacks. The worship service itself provides a meaningful shared experience that can draw people together and prompt discussion. Community milestones, issues, and events are often announced and prayed over during the service, sharing information that can draw the community closer. Sunday morning worship may incorporate several of the instituted means of grace like public prayer, searching scripture, and the Lord's Supper, each with the potential of sparking or strengthening the awareness of God's grace in individual worshippers.

Sunday morning worship also acts as a catalyst for the formation of sub-communities that address particular aspects of worship. Some congregants may come together as a choir, practicing during the week to provide music for services. A worship committee might come together to shape the particulars of the worship gathering, and an altar guild might work together to prepare the worship space each week. The larger gathering provides an opportunity for smaller groups to form with the purpose of allowing those with particular gifts, talents, or interests to utilize them in the service of the whole group. All of these subgroups have the potential to act as prudential means of grace, as they allow a person to exercise a personal gift or talent specifically in the service of God, which can be quite moving. A person who does not connect with God through the larger worship service might experience God's grace while practicing the choir anthem or while quietly arranging the altar flowers.

Sunday morning worship gatherings also provide the opportunity to gather for Sunday school, a time of communal Christian education. Sunday school classes gather before or after worship to study scripture or to discuss topics from a Christian perspective. They are often divided by gender, age, or marital status ostensibly to gather people of similar interests and life experience. Sunday school classes can often become strong communities as people share the experience of learning together and growing together over time. Because Sunday school classes often gather people at similar phases of life, members of a class may face similar problems and life stresses. That encourages the sharing of personal experience and the nurturing of people in crisis. A person whose spouse is suffering from cancer is likely to encounter a person who has had a similar experience within a Sunday school class, providing an avenue for God's grace to flow through the experienced person into the life of the suffering person.

Churches often sponsor Bible study groups. These typically meet at times other than those dedicated for Sunday school or worship. Bible study groups tend to meet for longer periods than Sunday school classes, and they tend to be more specifically focused on the in-depth study of scripture or a religious text. Bible study groups typically embody the instituted means of grace of searching scripture, the detailed and careful study of the Bible, and Christian conferencing, a conversation among people who are specifically focused on growing in holiness through the discussion of life and scripture. Bible study groups can form close community because of the aspect of mutual discovery and growth in holiness. As people work side by side to interpret and more deeply understand and appreciate scripture, they share the intimacy of growing in their love of God.

There are other types of groups that are similar to Bible study groups that can also produce strong community formation. Spiritual formation or inquiry groups are similar to Bible study groups but are focused on the study of spiritual leaders and spiritual practices. These groups may examine the works of Christian mystics or theologians, and they may study various forms of Christian prayer and meditation. The shared experience of discovery, insight, and spiritual growth can draw the participants closely together as they grow in holiness. These groups often dwell at the intersection of the instituted means of grace of public and private prayer as, together, they learn to pray more deeply. They can act as each other's guides as they learn and grow through God's grace.

Small groups are another form of gathering that can yield strong community. Similar to Bible studies or spiritual formation groups in that they usually center around the study of scripture or a book, small groups differ in that they tend to meet in members'

TOGETHER

homes in order to foster a more domestic and family-oriented feeling. In small groups, study is often subordinate to personal connection and interaction. Small groups are similar in many ways to the "class meetings" of early Methodism where groups of twelve would meet regularly as accountability and support groups. The traditional class meeting question, "How is it with your soul?" is not typically asked in contemporary small groups, but attention to spiritual and physical health is common. God's grace flows through these groups in the form of caring, love, and connection.

Churches often facilitate the formation of communities designed to help and serve others. Denominational entities facilitate mission and relief work, providing the local church with opportunities to connect through specialized training and financial donations. Local church members can train to participate in disaster relief or to act as child advocates in the judicial process. These opportunities foster personal connections throughout the world with those receiving aid or services and can diminish the sense of separation that some feel from people of other regions or countries. Similarly, local churches can participate in short-term mission trips, in which a group of people devote time and resources to fill a perceived need outside of the church itself. Short-term mission can involve travel, although that is not a necessity, but it always includes separating the mission team from their normal interpersonal connections and working environment. This separation can provide a catalyst for community formation within the group as people connect through the shared experience of service. Short-term mission can act as a means of grace by exposing the actions of God in an unfamiliar environment. It is very often the case that the blessings and graces received by the short-term missionaries can exceed those received by the recipients of the missionary assistance.

Groups emerge through feeding and crafting ministries established in or by churches. Close communities often form as people work together to use their talents and resources to meet others' needs. Groups that work together preparing and serving food for others often bond through the shared creative experience.

God's grace flows to them through what John Wesley referred to as "works of mercy,"[1] or actions taken to alleviate the physical needs of others. Similar communities can form as groups of people with sewing or crafting skills come together to make blankets, prayer shawls, quilts, and pillows for people in need or under stress. These crafting groups provide the shared experience of creation and focus on those in need, which can draw people together in love.

Churches are excellent venues for the formation of self-help and special interest groups, which can become means of grace. Church facilities are often used by 12-step groups that provide accountability and support to people seeking to heal from addictions or behavioral issues. These communities facilitate the flow of God's grace into troubled lives through making space for people to care for each other and through the language of spirituality and accountability. Churches can also gather people with a shared special interest, ranging from child-rearing to grief counseling to caring for aging parents. Churches are often uniquely positioned to invite vulnerable people into community with each other in a way that allows them to grow and learn together in a place that feels safe. Such groups can be conduits of God's grace through the creation of nurturing environments that provide information, support, and accountability. God can share God's love through the love of others.

While this list of communities that can act as means of grace within traditional churches is not exhaustive, it clearly illustrates how powerfully and productively churches can establish human bonds that facilitate and encourage the flow of God's grace into people's lives. The potential for communities like this within established churches requires that we not summarily dismiss the community-formation experience and history of established churches simply because churches are not as central to community formation in neighborhoods as they once were. As we work to find new ways for people to form community in a Christian context, we must not neglect the time-proven old ways.

1. Wesley, "On Zeal," 1.5.

Because these types of communities are familiar to many of us, they can also serve as helpful platforms from which to consider communities that have failed to live up to their potential as means of grace. In chapter 4, I mentioned the stereotypes that have grown up around Christianity that make it difficult for some people to even consider Christian community. These stereotypes have kernels of truth within them that those of us who are interested in forming and expanding forms of Christian community should be aware of.

The first stereotype is that Christians are very exclusive, refusing to accept certain types of people into their communities. This charge often arises around sexual orientation and race, but in truth it can extend to any outsider. Some of the class groups I have encountered have grown so close to each other that it was impossible for new people to join them. The result was that new church members would either form new class groups, which had the effect of dividing the church into discrete groups of closed cliques, or they would simply leave because they were not incorporated into the community life of the church. It is vitally important that Christian communities remain open, welcoming new people who may be beginning their journey to encounter the spiritual and those who are already walking that path but need a new community to belong to. Tackling the larger questions of race and orientation will require denominations to act, but accepting each individual, regardless of race or orientation, is the work of the local community.

Another stereotype is that Christians are heavily focused on rule-keeping. Much of this stereotype hinges on the orientation of the community's worship and teaching towards God's grace. If a community is focused on hellfire, damnation, sinfulness, and a vengeful God, it is likely to seem rule-based and condemning to those who seek to connect with the community. On the other hand, a community that emphasizes the presence of God's grace in the lives of all people and the forgiving nature of God is likely to seem more welcoming and less rule-based. This is not to say that a community's theology should shift arbitrarily in order to attract people. Rather, a community should be aware of how its theological stance affects the ability of people to become part of their community.

In some regions of the United States, Christians are stereotyped as politically conservative. While we were living in north-central Texas, my wife, Jay, had a friend who was quite conservative. When Jay mentioned in conversation that she's a Democrat, the friend was appalled. "But Jay," she exclaimed, "can you be a Democrat and be a Christian?" Her friend was completely serious, having embraced the stereotypes promulgated in her social circle. A community needs to be aware of its political stance and needs to consciously decide whether it intends to allow political issues to shape it. One option is to intentionally choose to embrace political diversity, deciding to invite all to be part of a community without regard to political stance. Such a stance requires a community to intentionally set aside litmus-test issues such as sexual orientation and abortion, which may be very difficult for some to do. A community should be aware of the impact of its political stance on its ability to welcome new members.

Christians are sometimes stereotyped as hateful. Unfortunately, there is plenty of historical fodder for those who wish to propagate that stereotype—too many times war, destruction, and division have been undertaken in the name of Christ or the church. Politicians are not above using the term "Christian" as the opposite of "Muslim" or some other group they wish to marginalize or demonize. Communities that seek to be inviting and open to all who wish to come must recognize this stereotype and intentionally stand against it.

I had the opportunity to meet with a group of women who have a quilting community that meets on a weekday afternoon in a church space. That day, they rushed to introduce me to "our new Hindu," a lovely woman of Indian ancestry who had joined the group. The community was thrilled to have a new member who offered them a glimpse into another culture, and they welcomed her with open arms. That group of women consciously set aside the opportunity to discriminate and chose the opportunity to embrace.

45

True Christian community in a traditional church environment can be powerful and life-giving. We at the Missional Wisdom Foundation have been working on the transformation of a church building in western North Carolina. This lovely neighborhood church had a very long history of service to its community, but in recent years it had dwindled to fewer than twenty-five members. The small church community was close-knit and was searching for creative ways to remain alive. When the Missional Wisdom Foundation proposed a very forward-looking renovation of the church building to encourage new forms of Christian community, the church members were very supportive. They looked beyond the changes that they would need to embrace and saw the opportunity to provide a lovely place for their grandchildren to form community as they once had. They set aside the possibility of being selfish or self-centered and instead embraced change to welcome new people. This even included redesigning and moving a "history room" that had been put together by a group of church women more than twenty-five years ago. Two of the current church leaders sorted through all the materials and oversaw the relocation of the room to a classroom near the sanctuary where more people could enjoy the historical documents and artifacts that date back into the nineteenth century. These women saw past the "sacred and untouchable" nature of that room and transformed it into a living testimony to the need for transformation and change in the life of the church. They chose to use the history and tradition of their church as an invitation to people they do not yet know to carry that church tradition into the future.

Questions for Reflection

1. Why are sanctuaries so important to many congregations?

2. Why is the choir often a strong community within a church?

3. Why are Sunday school classes often strong communities within a church?

4. Why does focusing on the needs of others draw people together?

5. Which of the stereotypes have you encountered? Are they true?

7

Workplace as Community

IT SEEMS THAT ONE need only turn on the television to appreciate the workplace as a community. Recent favorites like *Parks and Recreation*, *30 Rock*, and *The Office*, along with British comedies like *Are You Being Served?* and *Fawlty Towers* and classics like *Frasier*, *Ally McBeal*, and *Cheers*, examine the depth, width, and comedic value of workplace relationships. For many people, the workplace is the primary source of adult interaction. Acquaintances, friendships, and relationships can all develop within the workplace, and the workplace can anchor a strong sense of belonging and self-image. People often introduce themselves by saying their name and then describing their occupation.

Seeing the workplace community as a potential means of grace is initially difficult for some because it is not uncommon to encounter intentional barriers established between the two. Some workplaces, in reaction to distractions and proselytizing, literally prohibit religious or spiritual discussion or symbols. The United States Equal Employment Opportunity Commission has established a very specific set of federal rules and regulations regarding the wearing of religious clothing and the maintenance of religious grooming requirements in the workplace. The tension between workplace rules and religious requirements has made it necessary

for the EEOC to be specific about hijabs in health clubs and mes-
sianic Christian beards in places that require male employees to be
clean-shaven.

The separation between the workplace and the spiritual can
flow much deeper than workplace rules. Particularly in the United
States, the tradition of the separation of church and state can become a separation between church and workplace. The "religion"
of capitalism can encourage actions and behavior that is inconsis-
tent with the tenets of Christianity. I once had a friend at church
with whom I traveled on several short-term youth mission trips
as a chaperone. I admired his commitment, his attitude towards
the teenagers, and his willingness to invest his own vacation time
to make it possible for young people to have an inspiring mission
experience. As I got to know him better, I learned that he worked
as an engineer at the local plant of a large defense contractor. His
daily occupation was designing "anti-personnel" systems. I finally
got up the nerve to ask him, "How do you reconcile your closely
held Christian beliefs with the fact that your life's work is designing ways to more efficiently kill people?" He looked at me and said,
"Work is work," and left it at that. It was clear to me that he had
built a significant mental wall separating those two aspects of his
life. While not always that extreme, there is an American mentality
of "Business is business" that echoes "All is fair in love and war." I
have seen many examples of cutthroat business behavior in people
who attend church; it is as if their Christianity is checked at the
office door.

Given those obstacles, how can workplace communities be
established in such a way that they can act as a means of grace? One
answer stems from the fact that many businesses are decentral-
izing their workplaces through telecommuting. Recent statistics
indicate that around 25 percent of the U.S. workforce telecom-
mutes with some frequency.[1] This phenomenon has people working from kitchen tables, home offices, and coffee shops, which, in
turn, has caused many to seek alternative workplaces because of

1. As of January 2016. See http://globalworkplaceanalytics.com/telecom
muting-statistics.

the distractions and loneliness inherent in working from home. This has led to the advent of coworking spaces.

Coworking is a global movement to establish shared workspaces for people who want to work in a community environment that is encouraging and collaborative. Coworking is distinguished from other shared workspace concepts like executive suites and business incubators by its focus on community and collaboration. People who choose to work in coworking spaces do so precisely because they want the energy and insights of coworkers in their workspace. Coworking spaces usually have staff members who help make connections between the members and who coordinate programming for business and social enrichment. Coworking.com lists five core values that embody the spirit of coworking: community, openness, collaboration, sustainability, and accessibility.[2]

In 2015, the Missional Wisdom Foundation opened The Mix Coworking and Creative Space in the basement of White Rock United Methodist Church (WRUMC) in Dallas, Texas. WRUMC, under the leadership of Reverend Mitchell Boone and Neil Mosely, Director of Community Engagement, was transforming its church space to more deeply connect with its neighborhood. As a part of a comprehensive plan that included the establishment of a community garden, the incorporation of a neighborhood school, and the integration of a Buddhist meditation space, WRUMC leased its 15,000-square-foot basement to the Foundation. The space included a large community room, a stage, a kitchen, a few storerooms, and five cinderblock classrooms.

Working in concert with the church, Daryn DeZengotita, the Catalyst[3] of The Mix, began the process of decluttering the space. After the removal of years' worth of church detritus, the space was painted, new lighting was installed, and deferred maintenance was addressed. Daryn and Rhonda Sweet, the Conduit[4] of The Mix, oversaw the installation of a coffee bar, high-speed Internet, and a water bottle filling station. They purchased a variety of furniture

2. See http://blog.coworking.com/core-values/.
3. On-staff facilitator.
4. The Conduit oversees the kitchen and hospitality in The Mix.

from a discount warehouse store, secondhand stores, and a local artisan who makes tables from recycled industrial pallets. The result is a funky, functional, and friendly workspace.[5]

In its first year of operation, more than forty people joined The Mix. Some work for corporations and nonprofits, others are entrepreneurs or corporate refugees. They share a potluck lunch on Wednesdays, "TED + Tea at 10" on Thursdays, and a wide variety of business enrichment seminars and exercise classes each month. Most of The Mix's members live in the immediate neighborhood.

And The Mix works as a means of grace. I recently attended a Wednesday lunch there and was joined at the table by a young woman visiting a friend who is a member of The Mix. As we ate together, the young woman allowed that she had a serious health problem and was facing imminent surgery. We asked whether we could help her in any way, and she said, "Well, I am here because I just love the vibe here. Maybe you could just send me some good vibes." Someone at the table said, "Well, some of us call that prayer. Would it be okay if we prayed for you?" The young woman agreed, and several of us placed our hands on her head and shoulders and prayed for her and her medical team. She was obviously touched by this expression of love, and was grateful for the attention and the blessing. She had not come seeking prayer, but her spirit was touched by the Spirit of the place.

Daryn and Rhonda can tell dozens of similar stories ranging from coworkers supporting each other through a death in the family to a woman who broke down in tears when she entered a church sanctuary for the first time in years on her introductory tour. The Mix is not a "bait and switch" operation—members are not expected to attend worship and Sunday school, although a few of them have chosen to do so. They are expected to connect with their coworkers and to be encouraging and open to dialogue. The Mix is a "yes-and" space—a secular workspace in a sacred environment where interactions between those two are welcomed.

The church space that The Mix occupies has physical attributes that will be developed to further expand the coworking

5. Photos are online at http://themixcoworking.spaces.nexudus.com/en.

environment to include food preparation professionals as well as office workers. The kitchen in the space will be improved and renovated into a full shared-use kitchen where people who cater meals or make specialty items will be able to use a commercial kitchen. Many home kitchens do not meet the regulations required for selling food to the general public, so a commercial kitchen significantly broadens the markets they can address. The kitchen will be designed with a significant amount of preparation space that will allow members to teach classes in a comfortable and efficient environment.

The stage in the large space has been cleaned and reopened, allowing a local children's theater group to use it to practice and perform. One of the storage closets has been soundproofed and transformed into a podcasting studio. The physical resources of the church space have been refined to facilitate the growth of community in the coworking space.

One of the classroom spaces was converted to host the Ahadi Collective, an economic empowerment experiment facilitated by the Missional Wisdom Foundation. Ahadi is a textile collective run by a community of African refugees, many of whom worship in the Foundation's New Day missional micro-church in North Dallas. Ahadi produces clergy stoles, yoga pillows, and fabric shopping bags, seeking to use repurposed or fair-trade fabrics in order to be gentle with our planet. Ahadi means "promise" in Swahili and is the name chosen by the community as a reminder of God's promise to them. The Ahadi workers work and pray together, and earn income to support their families while developing and improving work skills in a grace-filled environment.

A number of local businesses have relocated into former classrooms. They have created specialized shared spaces needed for their businesses. A professional dance company installed mirrors and a dance floor in one classroom, which now functions as a practice and rehearsal space. The space is also available for use by a nonprofit that teaches dance to people with physical disabilities. Everyone in The Mix was blessed by a recent performance on The Mix stage featuring young women with spina bifida dancing on specially built wheeled carts with members of the professional dance company. Another classroom houses a textile arts business that offers weaving, knitting, and crochet classes together with a large inventory of earth-friendly and repurposed fabric. Yet another classroom accommodates a shared-use art studio with a floral business a local entrepreneur moved out of her kitchen. These relocated businesses add to the environment and vitality of The Mix through the creation of a wider variety of resources available to the community and an additional flow of creative people into the coworking environment.

One of the interesting sidebars of The Mix is that it has played an important role in empowering women. Daryn DeZengotita, the Catalyst of The Mix, describes our experience like this:

> In a little more than one year, The Mix has become a space where women, in particular, can find the support and collaborative spirit they need to build a business, explore new opportunities, or expand a dream. Some of our coworkers include
>
> - Melissa DeGroat, Creative Director of Epiphany DanceArts, who wanted to expand her professional dance company to include a social enterprise—teaching adaptive dance for special-needs children and young adults. Her special dancers weren't always welcome at other studios around town . . . including spaces in churches. The Mix has been a great fit for her—welcoming *all* of her dancers, connecting her with the church worship director, who will be live-drumming for their next event, and helping them promote their branding and marketing communications.
>
> - Kristi Kelley, owner of Stem and Style, who is typical of our coworkers who have worked from home but want to *reclaim* their home. When you live where you work, it's very difficult to draw boundaries around your work life and your family life. Also, our expansive space is allowing her to invest in a large floral cooler she needs to expand her business. She also hopes to become the in-house florist for the

church, and to collaborate with another member company—an event and wedding planner.

- Amy Margaret King, owner of Nested Strategies, who is establishing her own coworking space later this year. You heard that right—in the coworking movement, it makes perfect sense to collaborate with another company that others might see as competition. It is the way of the shared economy, and of women collaborating, in particular, to look for the whole that is "greater than the sum of its parts" rather than the zero-sum game. Amy's new space, GoodWork, will be a second space for Mixers, and vice versa, as we offer reciprocal privileges.

- The women of the Ahadi Collective, who are growing a commercial textiles concern in The Mix. They are African refugees with whom the Missional Wisdom Foundation has worked for a few years. They must always contend with the challenge of finding sustainable employment that supports their large families. One is a master seamstress who is training the others. Neighbors and collaborators have brought in piecework and projects *and* taken the time to train and coach the women to improve their skills in both sewing and marketing. A big win? One of the women was just offered a *better* job by one of their customers!

And so many more . . .

- Andra and Renae, who have realized their dream of a children's theater.

- Bonni, who has launched "Next Chapter" for accomplished women in the Third Act of their lives.

- Jen, who shared that her son was having some pretty significant coming-of-age issues and who found a listening ear and, much to her surprise, a pastor.

- Ronda, who was devastated by being forced to close a very successful business and is finding the inspiration and support to reinvent it.

- Lydia, who is struggling with the need to hold down a "real job" while her entrepreneur's heart is crying to be unleashed.

- Sandra, who, facing financial struggles, took a leap to teach basic kitchen skills and has had smashing success.

- Angela, who cares for two small children and cherishes her time in The Mix to connect with adults and keep her writing skills sharp. We were also a place of comfort for her when she lost a family member recently, an uncle who was the only member of her family who shared her Christian faith.

- Carissa, who is stepping out as a freelancer for the first time and loves the support she gets from others who have been there.

I'll stop myself here, but just know that I could go on! It's also important to note that the coworking movement is often criticized for being dominated by men—literally and figuratively. Our gender ratio is highly unusual!

I hope that these brief profiles will help you expand your concept of what "empowering women" can mean. In ways great and small, it's what we do #inTheMix!

Daryn recently shared another experience that illustrates the power of the workplace as a means of grace. In July 2016, a gunman ambushed and killed five Dallas police officers, wounding nine more before he was killed by the police using a bomb mounted on a remote bomb disposal robot. These are Daryn's words about that experience:

> The Dallas police shootings, and shootings of black men that precipitated the protest, really created a time of very deep conversation and connection in The Mix. We were all a little shell-shocked on that Friday and just sort of dumbfounded. But conversations opened up between black women and white women, as basic as black women fear things that white women don't, and how very, very sad that made us. And as challenging as being called to rethink my support for Chief David Brown's decision to

summarily execute the shooter was, it was an intense and sacred time as we simply made space for it.

An intense and sacred time. At work. In a church. At The Mix.

Questions for Reflection

1. How do you feel about businesses in church spaces?

2. Think about your best "workplace" friend. What drew you together? Are you friends outside of the workplace? Why or why not?

3. Could your church allow a group of refugees to run a business in your church space? Would it cause friction?

4. Could your church welcome groups of handicapped people into your church space? Is your space accessible? If not, how does that affect your ability to welcome all?

5. If a person simply works in a church space and only engages with the people in the workspace, how will they encounter the Holy Spirit? If the person is Christian, how will they grow as disciples?

7

Communities Formed Around Food

ONE OF THE OFT-REPEATED hallmarks of a missional life is "following the example of Jesus." The Gospel of Luke mentions six particular times that Jesus was in the synagogue or temple, including his presentation as an infant and his time with the elders as a child. The same Gospel mentions eleven specific instances when he was dining with others, including three times at the homes of Pharisees and once after the resurrection, following the walk to Emmaus. There are at least eleven more instances in Luke when Jesus uses food as an illustration or a teaching tool. And, of course, it was by means of a meal that Jesus chose to assure us of his continuing presence: the instituted means of grace that is the Lord's Supper. Remind me one more time how we concluded that one hour on Sunday morning should be the focus of our Christian life?

Growing, preparing, and sharing food can be powerful catalysts to the formation of strong communities. Gardening and farming are beautiful examples of the idea of "co-creation," in which our labors—our tilling, planting, weeding, and harvesting—combine with God's miracles of life and sustenance to produce fruits and vegetables that nourish us. Food preparation includes creativity and nurturing, and can transform the simple need for nourishment into an elemental pleasure. Sharing food together can be intimate, providing the opportunity for storytelling and connecting as we nourish our bodies. Because food is a basic human need, activities around food can touch people very deeply.

Gardening is a central activity at Haw Creek Commons (HCC), an adaptive reuse/transformation of Bethesda UMC in Asheville, North Carolina, being led by the Missional Wisdom Foundation. Under the leadership of Katey Rudd, the Cultivator at HCC, volunteers have transformed the suburban front yard of the church parsonage into a lush garden that produces corn, tomatoes, squash, zucchini, and other wonderful food. The produce is used to prepare meals for people who come to HCC for retreats, and it is shared with the neighbors and with the local food bank. Neighborhood volunteers care for the garden under Katey's guidance, which opens the door for the formation of community. Here is an example, in Katey's words:

> It was just before Christmas and I'd been invited by my friend Casey, one of the only people I know in Asheville, to go to a holiday craft exchange and potluck. I had been pumped for it for a few weeks: what a great way to get some holiday shopping done, get artisan gifts, and most of all, meet people! When the night came I felt like doing anything but going. I was exhausted and feeling my introvert bookworm coming on hard. I sat in my truck for a while debating whether I should go and begrudgingly decided it would be a good thing to do. I'm so very glad I did.
>
> I got to the house feeling awkward. I didn't know anyone but Casey, and she was talking privately in her room with a friend, so I started browsing homemade jewelry. A woman came up next to me and we spent about ten minutes helping each other narrow our many desired choices to one pair of earrings each. This prompted an hour and a half conversation about our stories.
>
> It turns out she and her husband of many years had recently divorced, and she had had to move from the three-acre farm they cultivated together. She expressed her pain and how terribly she missed having her hands in the dirt. Enter Haw Creek Commons! I had shared

about my life, but now I shared about my work and our vision for the space. She was stunned and jumped on the opportunity to volunteer to garden, plan with me, and teach the elementary students from Haw Creek Commons. (Aside: we have been planning to start a once-a-week gardening after-school program for kids and their parents, which has had an overwhelmingly positive response . . . but I need help!)

The woman expressed how healing it would be for her and how ecstatic she would be to become involved, and added that she lived less than ten minutes from the church!

Today I got the opportunity to give her a tour of the property, vision with her, discuss a project timeline, and introduce her to Karen (Rev. Karen Doucette is the Community Pastor at HCC). She was thrilled and kept saying, "I can't believe a church is actually doing all this. This is not how I think of churches. This is so amazing."

Not only am I unendingly grateful to have an experienced garden volunteer, but also to have, yet again, witnessed the power of just showing up and being available. Though she practices new age spirituality, she couldn't express enough how much healing she would find at Haw Creek Commons and how supportive of the vision she was. She begins yoga teacher training this Friday as well, and has already said a big "Yes" to teaching classes at HCC once construction is complete!

In addition to the front-yard garden, Katey has coordinated the installation of several beehives in the backyard, providing a small army of pollinators for the garden and a wonderful source of honey and bee's wax. She has plans for the construction of several keyhole gardens on the path between HCC and the local elementary school adjacent to the church so that the children can enjoy watching food grow. Katey and Karen Doucette are working with the elementary school administration to design a set of enrichment experiences for the students, all focused on the gardens. They have already hosted groups of students to work and harvest in the garden, to watch the beekeeper tend the bees, and to play with the worms in the vermiculture composter.

Shared-use commercial kitchens can host a specialized type of coworking community. People who run small catering businesses or who produce specialty foods from their homes can share access to a licensed commercial kitchen, making it possible for them to sell their goods to a much larger market and to form friendships and connections at the same time. Both HCC and The Mix will include fully equipped shared-use commercial kitchens that will incorporate a significant amount of preparation and teaching space. Rhonda will lead the shared kitchen at The Mix, utilizing her experience as a well-recognized chef and caterer. Katey will enliven the kitchen at HCC, relying on her training as a registered dietitian and holistic wellness coach. The kitchens will act both as food-production facilities and as teaching venues. Brian Good, an Asheville-based restaurateur and restaurant broker, worked with the Foundation to design the kitchen at Haw Creek. He testified on behalf of the project to the Asheville City Council as part of a zoning hearing for HCC:

> Haw Creek Commons Community Kitchen is an oppor-
> tunity to take an underutilized space and make it a place
> where the community, charity groups, and small business
> can prepare, cook, and package food items for the com-
> munity. It is a place where everyday learning, fellowship,
> and entrepreneurship can thrive. Haw Creek Commons
> is an opportunity for small business to survive in a mar-
> ket where margins are slim and the competition is fierce.
>
> When I was invited to Haw Creek Commons to first
> look at the space, I was intrigued with the vision to create
> a space where food-service professionals can collaborate
> in a shared-use kitchen. Small food-based businesses
> have a hard time coming up with the capital to build
> a space to safely prepare food. Many small food-based
> businesses take a risk by starting in their uninspected
> homes or paying all their profits to rent a space. Haw
> Creek Commons wanted to provide a safe, clean, in-
> spected, modern, up-to-date kitchen for these small
> food-based businesses or nonprofit groups to prepare,
> cook, and package their products. After my first visit I
> knew that I had to be a part of this project!

I was able to help start the GO-Kitchen Ready program at Green Opportunities with Mark Rosenstein and learned firsthand of the challenges for people who have transportation or childcare issues while starting a business. We have one shared-use kitchen at the Blue Ridge Food Ventures that focuses on freeing up profits, which is out on the western edge of Buncombe County, which limits access for residents of other regions. Haw Creek Commons will allow residents of the east side of Buncombe County access to a certified commercial kitchen.

My wife and I started up her business, Tiffany's Baking Co., eight years ago at a shared-use commercial kitchen. We were able to grow the business and create a successful operation that has contributed to the area. We would have not been able to realize our dreams if not for an opportunity like Haw Creek Commons. This space has the potential for positively affecting many lives, families, and businesses for the better, by allowing people to realize their dreams.

Table fellowship has been a traditional part of the life of many Christian denominations for years in the form of Wednesday night dinners or Friday fish fries. These activities, however, were typically inwardly focused—serving the people of the church—and were large gatherings. Lynda Fickling, director of servant ministry and spiritual director at St. Luke's UMC in Highlands Ranch, Colorado, and a graduate of the MWF's Launch & Lead program, decided to combine the joys of table fellowship with the idea of small groups by developing Kitchen Groups. Lynda put together a leader's guide that provided insight into hosting a simple dinner in a home. She emphasized inviting neighbors, especially those in need. She discouraged overpreparation and showing off, suggesting simple foods and a hospitable environment. Her guide suggested the sharing of stories and gave examples of prayers and liturgies that might be incorporated into the dinners. She also provided a few resources on table fellowship from academic sources to broaden the imaginations of the group leaders. The entire guide was seven pages long.

And then Lynda began a group in her own home. This is how she describes what happened:

> We usually simply gather to share a meal, share our life stories, encourage one another, and share devotion, prayer, and communion. Very simple—with no structure. I have found giving new leaders "structure" is helpful when newly forming, but I remind them to leave room for the Spirit and go where that leads them . . . which is, after a few times, very loose.
>
> My group has been together now for five years this fall. We have been through a death of one member, a death of one member's son, two divorces, new jobs, and many spiritual challenges and journeys. We took the summer off because so many were scattered, but we are starting up in September. We are planning to meet once a month. Personally, I am truly blessed to have each one of them in my life—God put us together for many reasons!
>
> Our church offered these as "Kitchen Groups"—one of our many *Communitas* offerings for the fall last year. We encouraged them to continue but did have a six-week, once-a-week format that was offered in two sessions. So, we had around forty-eight people meeting in the fall. Two groups have continued to meet. They all seemed to enjoy the concept and I hope are continuing to invite "others" to their tables. One didn't work because they were on a Sunday early evening and, well . . . Broncos football is our competition! One group was a vegan group; not all were vegan, but they were there to learn what that was and how to cook these foods! Also, a key is to rotate homes—if you keep it in only one home or host, it seems to lose the meaning of opening your home to the other.

Simple foods are an important aspect of groups like these. It seems that church potluck dinners sometimes devolve into cooking competitions to see whose chicken and dumplings recipe is best or who makes the best pineapple upside-down cake. The MWF facilitates a missional micro-church called New Day in North Dallas, and their time together always begins with a simple meal. The rule of thumb at New Day is that any member of the congregation should be capable of bringing any food item that is provided. Because many of the congregants are refugees who do not have much money, this rule yields lots of beans, soups, and salads—healthy fare that all can enjoy. Simple foods remind us of God's bountiful abundance while also reminding us that our actual needs are often not quite as extravagant as our "wants." The garden is full of good food.

Lynda's "Kitchen Groups" are creative, informal, and fun. They create an atmosphere where love can grow, and where people can learn to care for each other and to grow together. They make space for prayer and communion in a way that builds the spiritual connection between the participants.

They are a means of grace.

Questions for Reflection

1. How would Sunday worship change if the service included a community meal?

2. How is a community gardening experience different when there is a single garden that everyone works on versus individual plots assigned to specific people?

3. Why is gardening invitational?

4. Why do shared-use commercial kitchens make economic sense?

5. How do Kitchen Groups differ from traditional small groups?

8

Communities Formed Around Children's Schools and Activities

IN DECEMBER 2015, THE Pew Research Center released a fascinating study called "Parenting in America: Outlook, worries, aspirations are strongly linked to financial situation."[1] Researchers surveyed 1,807 U.S. parents with children younger than eighteen. Here are some of the researchers' observations:

- The number of single-parent households grew from 9 percent in 1960 to 26 percent in 2014.

- Eighty-four percent of parents surveyed sometimes feel rushed. Thirty-one percent always feel rushed.

- Fifteen percent say their child's schedule is too hectic.

- Quality, affordable childcare is hard to find, according to 62 percent of respondents. Fifty-seven percent of households with income less than $30,000 rely on family members for childcare.

- Among school-age children, 73 percent have participated in sports, 60 percent in religious education or youth groups,

1. Pew Research Center, December 17, 2005, http://www.pewsocialtrends.org/files/2015/12/2015-12-17_parenting-in-america_FINAL.pdf.

54 percent in music, art, or dance lessons, and 53 percent in some form of volunteer work. Children in families with incomes of less than $30,000 are much less likely to participate.

- Forty-six percent of parents surveyed say they wish they could do more in their children's lives.

- Sixty-two percent of parents surveyed say they are overprotective sometimes, while 25 percent say they give too much freedom sometimes.

- Among millennials (ages eighteen to thirty-four), 43 percent of fathers and 57 percent of mothers say they are doing a very good job as a parent.

- Lower-income parents are much more concerned about the personal safety of their children.

- Lower-income parents are much more likely to describe their neighborhoods as "fair" or "poor" places to raise children.

These observations shed an interesting light on the importance of community formation around children's schools and recreational activities. Especially in low-income neighborhoods, safe and low-cost after-school activities are very important to parents who cannot afford many extracurricular activities and who are concerned about the safety of their children. Extracurricular activities are important in children's lives because they provide enrichment that is not available during the school day, and religiously related activities are popular avenues for these activities. Curriculum pressures have pushed music, art, and many sports out of the school and into the realm of the extracurricular. Parents are very involved in their children's activities, with many wishing they could do even more. Many parents feel that their lives are very hectic, so activities close to home are attractive.

Churches have historically recognized youth groups and Christian education for children as a very important role of the church. Mission trips designed for teens and families can be formative life experiences, as can church-sponsored summer camps. Vacation Bible School is another historically well-established program of the church that provides fun and education for children while giving caregivers a break in the summer. There are many possibilities for bringing people together around school and kid's activities.

When we were in the early phases of the Haw Creek Commons project in Asheville, several of us spent time sitting in lawn chairs in the church parking lot, simply talking with folks and watching the flow of people in the neighborhood. As we watched, it became obvious that the traffic around our local elementary school, which is immediately adjacent to the church property, was simply terrible at pick-up and drop-off times. The line of cars snaked all the way down the long school driveway into the narrow street in both directions, snarling traffic on several nearby streets. We also noticed that a few folks would either walk from their homes or drive to the church parking lot to walk across the backyard of the church to pick up their children. People seemed quite sheepish about parking in the church lot, pretty clearly concerned that we were going to fuss at them about taking up our holy spaces. Several of us realized that we had an opportunity to relieve a neighborhood problem.

So, we set out to intentionally invite people to use the church to avoid the carpool line. We put up metal street signs in the church parking lot inviting people to park there to pick up their children. We are working to install a walkway across the church yard to the school, making it easier to walk in all weather conditions, and we are planning keyhole gardens along the path so everyone can enjoy watching food grow and share in the produce. We installed a nice, simple swing set in the grassy yard, cleared out a play area in the woods, and placed four picnic tables near the playground for parents and caregivers. We even installed a Little Free Library[2] next to the parking lot so families could borrow books. With a little attention and a small investment, a warm and inviting environment was created for our neighbors. On a pretty day, it is not unusual to

---

2. A Little Free Library is a small, weathertight enclosure where books are made available to passersby. The idea is that the reader will leave a book as well, thus keeping the flow of books fresh.

see twenty people outside in that space—little kids on the swings, big kids running in the woods, and parents and caregivers chatting at the picnic tables. Karen and Katey are pretty intentional about finding time to sit out there too, often with a basket of produce, fresh fruit, or cookies, simply to extend hospitality and to get to know the neighbors. People who used to worry about sneaking across the church property now feel welcomed, and neighbors are connecting with each other in a comfortable space created by a Christian community.

Careful observation also called an issue to the attention of Daryn and Rhonda at The Mix. They noticed that the summer-school schedule placed extra stress on many Mix members as they struggled to arrange childcare for their kids. The Mix is kid-friendly, with dedicated play space stocked with creative toys and art supplies, but that space was not a substitute for supervised childcare for an extended period. Daryn and Rhonda worked with a Mix member who runs an on-site childcare service for special events, to form MixKids, a low-cost series of fun, supervised activities for children during the workday. The Mix team sees the availability of good childcare as a social-justice issue, as they are very aware that an inability to provide a safe and nurturing environment for children can derail the ability of a parent to work.

In her role as Community Pastor at Haw Creek Commons, Karen intentionally finds time to connect with the area schools and sports activities. She volunteers as a reading mentor at the elementary school and she attends local little-league baseball and basketball games. Her biggest commitment is acting as the coach of the girl's tennis team at the local high school. That role has given her the ability to really connect with a group of girls and with their parents in a way that is simply not traditional for a pastor. She is able to model Christian behavior in a competitive environment without needing to preach or proselytize. For her girls and their parents, the stereotype of Christian and pastor has been replaced by the smile and patience of Coach Karen.

Haw Creek Commons is a wonderful venue for extracurricular activities that connect kids and families. Here is an example, in Katey's words:

> Our first event was called Sole Hope, and we passed out 250 flyers to elementary school students inviting them and their families to participate. Together we cut shoe patterns out of old blue jeans brought by students or purchased at thrift stores. The patterns will be sent to Uganda, where native Ugandan women are paid a living wage to sew and assemble them with rubber soles and a strap to create shoes for Ugandan children whose feet are plagued by sand fleas. Sand flea bites cause immense pain, often preventing children from standing, sometimes making amputation necessary, and even leading to death. The simple act of wearing shoes almost entirely prevents this problem. (For more information, see www. solehope.org.)
>
> We had a showing of eleven children, all first and third-graders, and two parents. We played the Sole Hope video and it piqued the kids' curiosity: they asked if we could Google the sand fleas so they could learn what the fleas and bites looked like. After a flurry of cutting, painting, making an additional Christmas craft, and eating snacks, we let the kids play on the playground and make hot chocolate as parents and younger siblings trickled in.
>
> There were several conversations of particular note. One of the first moms who came to pick up pulled me aside and said something to the effect of, "Thank you so much for doing this. You know, I wasn't raised with any religion at all and don't really know if I believe there is a God or not . . . I just don't know anything about it; however, my daughter [a first-grader] has been asking a lot about God and church and I just don't know what to say to her or how to answer her questions. Would you all be willing to talk with her? Maybe you could even do something once a month and even if she is the only one that comes, I'll be grateful. I just don't know how to talk with her about it, and . . . I don't really know what I'm asking . . ." I replied to her, "Well, maybe you are trying to facilitate her exploring. That's so good!" She responded,

"Yes, that's what I want! I want to facilitate that. It would be so great if you or the pastor could talk with her." They stayed for roughly a half hour afterward, children playing and mom chatting with other moms.

The interesting thing about this encounter was that we very intentionally presented this as an a-religious event, creating a flyer with Haw Creek Commons as the sponsor, not Church, and creating a neutral space downstairs without a lot of very overtly religious messages and icons. We didn't pray and didn't mention anything other than the Sole Hope information and Christmas craft, yet this was the first thing the mom said to us. What is beautiful about this to Karen and me is that we literally just provided Presence: made ourselves and our space available. This alone sparked curiosity and conversation. Many folks are immediately put off by what sounds like "evangelizing" and this was a beautiful example of setting up a blank canvas, letting the Spirit control the situation, and watching the people of the community begin to paint. Instead of leading with what may sound like a "sales pitch for Jesus" we led with availability, service, and building community. This was a glimpse to us of what it looks like to actively rest in trust. It also encouraged us about the potential power of the space.

The second story was an exchange I overheard. A mother was picking up her child and as he bent to pick up his backpack to leave she asked the first-grader, "Did you have fun?" To this he immediately replied, "Mom, did you know there are kids my age in the other part of the world that don't have shoes? Did you know bugs live in their feet and sometimes they can't walk? We got to help them today!" It impressed us that *this* was his takeaway—not the playground, fun painting craft, hot chocolate, or snacks. He got the message, felt the weight of it, and *that* is what he said when asked if he had fun.

This was such a powerful indicator to me: people, young and old, are hungry for meaning, for purpose. Our pure, essential nature is to see and care for other life forms.

TOGETHER

The creation of community around children's schools and activities fills an important need for connection in the lives of many people. Because many extracurricular activities are expensive or require incredible investments of time, local activities that are fun and educational are welcomed by students and parents alike. If those activities are held in a nurturing environment and led by positive and welcoming people, the potential for a positive experience by the student and parent is high. For many people, their children are the most important factor in their lives, so building community in a way that nurtures kids and feeds adults is a welcome and life-giving addition to daily life.

Questions for Reflection

1. Why are high-quality, low-cost after-school activities important to low-income parents?

2. Remember your fondest memory of an after-school activity. Could it have been a Christian community?

3. Imagine a casual meeting place on your church grounds similar to the one described at Haw Creek Commons. Could it gather people who are currently not part of your church community?

4. Does your church accommodate children at adult activities?

5. How do educational activities for children create community for adults?

9

Communities Formed
around Affinity Groups

SOMETIMES THERE IS GREAT power in doing individual activities in a group.

Several years ago, I had the opportunity to spend a week with the Taizé Community in eastern France. That wonderful ecumenical monastic community opens its doors to thousands of young people every year and steeps them in beautiful meditative song and prayer. Worship is held in the Church of Reconciliation, a cavernous open space with an altar at one end. Worshippers sit on the floor, with hundreds of people typically attending each service. One evening, we entered into an extended time of silence as is typical in Taizé worship, and I closed my eyes and settled into my quiet, inward-looking meditative stance. On that evening, however, I became aware of something very different. I started to listen to the silence and I could hear the people around me breathing. I heard the rustling of clothing as people shifted to remain comfortable and I heard the occasional cough or sneeze that is inevitable when large groups try to be quiet. I was overwhelmed by the sense that although I was alone in my thoughts and prayers, I was also part of a much larger community of thought and prayer. I thought of the body of Christ, and of being part of the communion of saints. My individual activity was very spiritually fruitful because I did it within a community.

There is something inherently wonderful about sharing fun with other people. Many people enjoy spending their recreational time with others, enhancing their pleasure from a particular activity by changing it into a shared experience. Some activities like team sports require a group of people to participate, while other more solitary ventures like hiking or woodworking can be done individually within a group. Almost any activity can be the stimulus for community formation.

Some churches have traditionally recognized the community-building aspects of sports through recreational ministries such as softball and basketball leagues. It is also not unusual for groups to form within churches around sewing, knitting, or quilting. At Bethesda UMC, in Asheville, a small group of neighborhood women meet each week to quilt and to sew pillows for the local VA hospital. As part of the Haw Creek Commons renovation of the church, we converted the basement of the parsonage into a quilting and sewing room. We installed bright LED lighting, strong shelving, sturdy tables, and a small kitchenette to create a comfortable space for them to gather and work. The space itself is flexible enough to be shared by other textile groups. The Mix also features textile spaces, including the Ahadi sewing room discussed in chapters 6 and 7. Both sharing a creative task for the benefit of others and learning a new creative skill can be wonderful sources of community bonding.

Nora Ortiz Fredrick is a consultant, fund-raiser, and entrepreneur in Anchorage, Alaska. Nora, a graduate of the Missional Wisdom Foundation's Launch & Lead program, noticed that the timing of traditional church services makes very little sense in Alaska. Many people are drawn to Alaska by its natural beauty and the wide variety of outdoor activities it offers, yet churches were asking people to take several hours out of the very middle of their weekends to come into an urban setting in order to sit indoors for worship. Nora chose instead to bring church to where the people wanted to be by founding Ascent Alaska. She gathered groups of people for hiking, biking, and fishing, and walked with them into God's beautiful creation. Nora lived into the observation that the Apostle Paul makes in the first chapter of the Letter to the Romans: "Ever since the creation of the world, God's invisible qualities—God's eternal power and divine nature—have been clearly seen, because they are understood through the things God has made" (Rom 1:20). Nora shepherded the group as they encountered God in nature, and walked alongside them as they unpacked spiritual encounters together. Church leaders had a hard time embracing the community because it differed so substantially from their understanding of church, but Ascent Alaska met for more than three years, touching and nurturing dozens of people.

Reverend Mary Beth Taylor noticed a different kind of community while she was Associate Pastor at Littleton UMC outside of Denver. Mary Beth, also a graduate of Launch & Lead, noticed that many people enjoyed spending some of their recreational time having a cold beer and some appetizers at the local pub, just like she and her life partner, Steve. She pulled together a small group of people and formed Open Space, a community that meets monthly in a local bar and grill. They describe their goal of "striving to be an open-minded group that invites all to spark deep conversation and find spiritual meaning in a safe and diverse environment, exchange insights without judgment, and find the small ways to help better our local and world communities." Under the guidance of a lead team of community members, Open Space discusses contemporary spiritual issues like "Sports & Spirituality" and "Angels and Demons and Mental Illness." The community is open and affirming, intentionally incorporating people of any orientation or background. Supportive denominational leadership has made it possible for Mary Beth's pastoral appointment to be completely focused on Open Space, embracing the possibilities of a thriving church community outside of the walls of the church building.

The possibilities for forming communities around shared recreational activities are practically limitless. By the time Haw Creek Commons and The Mix are fully completed, they will include spaces dedicated to quilting, sewing, woodworking, ceramics, pottery, knitting, gardening, cooking, canning, beekeeping, painting, and flower arranging. That long list does not even touch on the possibilities represented by individual outdoor and team sports and activities. The imagination seems to be the only limit.

Shared recreation is not the only form of affinity that can call people into community. One of the very first communities to enter Haw Creek Commons was a local 12-step group who let themselves into the quilting room once weekly to share stories and to support each other in their quest for sobriety. These wonderful people needed a space to gather in a quiet and confidential environment to do the hard work of helping each other.

Affinity groups of all kinds can gather in a way that leads to God. People who share a concern for a group of their neighbors or who seek to address a particular injustice or who share a medical condition can all gather to build bonds of love and concern for each other and for their neighbors. A welcoming space is often all that is required to allow these groups to form.

Communities formed around affinities require special attention to intentionally focus on God. It is easy to get drawn into the excitement of play, relaxation, and enjoyment, or into the pain and concern of a commonly held mission or experience, and to miss the presence of the Spirit in its midst. One helpful tool is an orientation toward gratitude. Community is a gift from God, and helping people be grateful for that gift draws attention to its source. I have found that the old phrase "Thanks be to God," or a simple "Thanks, God," can be all it takes to initiate a moment of quiet reflection.

Questions for Reflection

1. Why does quilting lend itself to community formation?

2. How do activities like sewing, canning, and woodworking lend themselves to the formation of intergenerational community?

3. How do common experiences like having cancer work to create community?

4. Name an affinity group that is not discussed in this chapter. Could it foster Christian community?

5. How can hiking foster Christian community? How can sharing a beer and conversation foster Christian community?

6. Is forming community around shared recreational activities expensive?

10

Evangelism, Discipleship, Imagination, and Courage

WE HAVE ONLY SCRATCHED the surface of the thousands of possibilities for alternative Christian community that present themselves when you realize that practically any community can act as a means of grace. The role of the leader of the community shifts from preaching, teaching, and officiating to interpreting, guiding, and helping people recognize the Holy Spirit in their midst. The traditional roles of the pastor are still important within the traditional church because the word must still be preached and sacraments rightly delivered, but the centrality of those roles shifts when the nature of the community changes. Pastoral leaders must be trained in community development and spiritual direction as well as in leading a Sunday service, and a new generation of ordained and lay leaders must emerge who are capable of organizing and leading these new forms of Christian community.

As you ponder the possibilities of coworking spaces, community gardens, and sewing collectives, you may be wondering, "What about the Great Commission?" Matthew 28:18–20 is very clear about making disciples and spreading the gospel, and, as a United Methodist, I can't go too long without "making disciples of Jesus Christ for the transformation of the world" ringing in my ears. How do evangelism and disciple-making work in the context of these alternative forms of Christian community?

First, a brief note. My perspective on evangelism and disciple-making flows from my Wesleyan theology. If that is not your theological stance, please read on to see how this works for me. An understanding of salvation through Jesus Christ with the flow of God's grace into peoples' lives is absolutely vital. Without a clear view of how these communities can help bring people into unity with God through Jesus Christ, it is unlikely that the new communities will ever amount to anything more than a community center. The world does not need more coffee shops and handmade quilts—it needs more people joined with God in a healthy and life-giving way.

John Wesley described his understanding of the process of salvation in a sermon entitled "The Scripture Way of Salvation." In this sermon, Wesley observes that humanity is separated from God. Through prevenient grace—grace that flows from God into people before they have a relationship with Christ—people begin to realize that a relationship with God is missing from their lives. In a beautiful ballet of call and response, the Holy Spirit emanates grace and people respond to that grace, moving closer to God. As people grow closer to God, they become aware of their need for Christ, and the Spirit offers pardon and acceptance through justifying grace. With the offer made and responded to, the ballet continues through the sanctifying grace of the Spirit. God continues to pour grace into the life of the person, and the person's response to grace draws the person closer to God in a lifelong process of sanctification and growing holiness. The dance of sanctification— God's grace and a person's response—leads to unity with God.

Within that framework, it is possible to see evangelism as working with the Spirit through prevenient grace with people who have not experienced justification, and to see disciple-making as working with the Spirit through sanctifying grace with people who have experienced justification. As people of God, we cannot "save" other people—that is the work of the Holy Spirit through Jesus

Christ with a willing response from the person—but we can work to bring people together in a way that makes it easier for them to encounter the grace of God in an environment that is encouraging, with people who can help interpret their experiences.

Practically any form of Christian community can act as a means of prevenient grace. As people come together to work, play, cook, or chaperone, they can encounter God's love through the people in their community. They can be touched as they serve others, they can witness acts of kindness in the lives of their coworkers, and they can watch Christian leaders respond to the needs of the people around them. They can have positive experiences in a church space, working to overcome the impact of stereotypes and previous damaging experiences. They can connect with Christian people who are not giving them pamphlets, pushing for donations, or pushing them into Sunday school.

The same observation holds true for Christian community as a means of sanctifying grace. God will touch the lives of people growing in holiness through inviting them into new kinds of community with new people. Those who have left the church because of apathy or time constraints or bad experiences can associate with communities that connect with real needs in their lives and thus reenter a relationship with other Christians; God's grace will flow from the hands, feet, and words of those around them, nurturing them through friendship, fellowship, and love.

It is very important to remember that the prudential means of grace provided through alternative Christian communities are *additional* means of grace, not *replacement* means of grace. People who connect through these communities will benefit from other prudential means of grace, and I believe that they must ultimately engage with instituted means of grace to grow in their relationship with God. We have watched people be touched by God's grace in The Mix and at Haw Creek Commons who have then chosen to connect with Sunday worship experiences at White Rock UMC and Bethesda UMC. Each of those congregations has welcoming, inclusive pastors and staff members, which makes the transition easier for those reentering a congregation after a long absence.

However, reincorporation into the worshipping community of a traditional church is not a goal of an alternative Christian community, and many will connect with an alternative Christian community who will never connect with the traditional church community. Therefore, it is essential to consider ways to introduce the instituted means of grace into alternative Christian communities in ways that are compatible with their community life. Inviting a community member to a church Bible study may be scary and off-putting for someone who has had a bad experience with traditional church or Bible-thumping criticism, but that same person might be interested in exploring the Bible's stance on current issues with a group of community members in the community space. Going to the sanctuary on Sunday morning to receive communion might be totally alien to some, so a Christian coworking space we know in Dallas has a "Wine-down Wednesday" activity with fresh bread and good wine, and the only caveat is that you may not serve yourself! A Wednesday prayer meeting may seem weird to some, while a class on Christian meditation may seem interesting and inviting. The instituted means of grace—prayer, searching scripture, the Lord's Supper, baptism, fasting, and Christian conferencing—are powerful, wonderful ways for God's grace to enter people's lives, so they must not be set aside. They must be translated into practices and offerings that make sense in people's lives today just as Christian community must be, so that those who have turned away from traditional church can enjoy the bounty that God has provided.

Which is why strong and imaginative leadership is critical to the success of alternative Christian community. My denomination requires a specialized master's degree and a rigorous two-year apprenticeship before a person can be ordained as an Elder in Full Connection, and the requirements for other denominations are often as demanding. We feel that we must have highly trained individuals to lead worship and that we need an expensive piano or good organ to supplement the audio system for great music and good preaching. Yet, for some reason, we feel like the community garden must be run completely by volunteers, and hiring a staff member to facilitate alternative Christian communities is an unobtainable budgetary nightmare. Alternative Christian communities are not an afterthought or an add-on—they are vital components of ministry for this century. In order to be successful, they need to be guided by leaders, both lay and clergy, who are trained and committed. Financial resources must be dedicated to creating and maintaining them. New mindsets must be embraced regarding charging rent and paying taxes and selling products so that these ministries can pay for themselves. Leaders must be allowed to engage in bivocational and other alternative ways of earning a living.

We need to free our imaginations and the imaginations of those around us. The work of bringing people into unity with God is the work of the Holy Spirit, and it is the work of each individual to respond. The Holy Spirit will do that work whether or not we are imaginative, but it is our job to bring as many as we can into connection with God's grace. We need to let our imaginations soar as we think of new types of community and new ways to connect with and serve people so that the means of grace are present wherever they possibly can be. We need to hold our past practices gratefully but lightly, to be well informed by tradition and at the same time free to grow and change.

And that will require courage. Embracing new kinds of Christian community changes the ways that we get paid and the ways we collect revenues. New types of community change the ways we measure success and they change what the church looks like. Many of our experiments will fail and will cost money. We will need to set out without a backpack or an extra shirt or sandals or a walking stick. We will need to have faith that God will provide.

And God will provide. The traditional church is not reaching people as it once did, and the Holy Spirit is unwilling to sit idly by as what once was fades away. The Spirit is on the move everywhere, bringing new vitality to the old structures and bringing entirely new forms of Christian community to life in far-flung places. The lost sheep are being brought back into the fold in new and exciting ways.

Don't be afraid. My love is stronger.

TOGETHER

My love is stronger than your fear.
Don't be afraid. My love is stronger.
And I have promised, promised to be always near.[1]

---

1. "Don't Be Afraid," by John Bell.

Questions for Reflection

1. Are alternative Christian communities capable of "making disciples"? If so, how?

2. How would you introduce the Lord's Supper into an alternative Christian community?

3. How would you introduce the study of scripture into an alternative Christian community?

4. Are financial worries an obstacle for you in trying something new?

5. What is your biggest obstacle to forming an alternative Christian community in your context?

Bibliography

The Book of Discipline of the United Methodist Church, 2012. Nashville: United Methodist Publishing House, 2012.

Duggins, Larry. *Simple Harmony: Thoughts on Holistic Christian Life*. Southlake: Columkille, 2012.

Maddox, Randy L. *Responsible Grace: John Wesley's Practical Theology*. Nashville: Kingswood, 1994.

Outler, Albert C., ed. *The Works of John Wesley*. Nashville: Abingdon, 1995.

Rusch, William G., trans. and ed. *The Trinitarian Controversy*. Philadelphia: Fortress, 1980.